Technologies for Learning Outside the Classroom

John A. Niemi, *Editor*
Northern Illinois University

Dennis D. Gooler, *Editor*
Northern Illinois University

NEW DIRECTIONS FOR CONTINUING EDUCATION
GORDON G. DARKENWALD, *Editor-in-Chief*
Rutgers University

ALAN B. KNOX, *Consulting Editor*
University of Wisconsin

Number 34, Summer 1987

Paperback sourcebooks in
The Jossey-Bass Higher Education Series

Jossey-Bass Inc., Publishers
San Francisco • London

John A. Niemi, Dennis D. Gooler (eds.).
Technologies for Learning Outside the Classroom.
New Directions for Continuing Education, no. 34.
San Francisco: Jossey-Bass, 1987.

New Directions for Continuing Education
Gordon G. Darkenwald, *Editor-in-Chief*
Alan B. Knox, *Consulting Editor*

Copyright © 1987 by Jossey-Bass Inc., Publishers
and
Jossey-Bass Limited

Copyright under International, Pan American, and Universal
Copyright Conventions. All rights reserved. No part of
this issue may be reproduced in any form—except for brief
quotation (not to exceed 500 words) in a review or professional
work—without permission in writing from the publishers.

New Directions for Continuing Education is published quarterly
by Jossey-Bass Inc., Publishers (publication number USPS 493-930).
Second-class postage paid at San Francisco, California, and at
additional mailing offices. POSTMASTER: Send address changes to
Jossey-Bass Inc., Publishers, 433 California Street, San Francisco,
California 94104.

Editorial correspondence should be sent to the Editor-in-Chief,
Gordon G. Darkenwald, Graduate School of Education, Rutgers
University, 10 Seminary Place, New Brunswick, New Jersey 08903.

Library of Congress Catalog Card Number LC 85-644750

International Standard Serial Number ISSN 0195-2242

International Standard Book Number ISBN 1-55542-961-0

Cover art by WILLI BAUM

Manufactured in the United States of America

Ordering Information

The paperback sourcebooks listed below are published quarterly and can be ordered either by subscription or single copy.

Subscriptions cost $48.00 per year for institutions, agencies, and libraries. Individuals can subscribe at the special rate of $36.00 per year *if payment is by personal check.* (Note that the full rate of $48.00 applies if payment is by institutional check, even if the subscription is designated for an individual.) Standing orders are accepted.

Single copies are available at $11.95 when payment accompanies order. (California, New Jersey, New York, and Washington, D.C., residents please include appropriate sales tax.) For billed orders, cost per copy is $11.95 plus postage and handling.

Substantial discounts are offered to organizations and individuals wishing to purchase bulk quantities of Jossey-Bass sourcebooks. Please inquire.

Please note that these prices are for the academic year 1986-87 and are subject to change without notice. Also, some titles may be out of print and therefore not available for sale.

To ensure correct and prompt delivery, all orders must give either the *name of an individual* or an *official purchase order number.* Please submit your order as follows:

Subscriptions: specify series and year subscription is to begin.
Single Copies: specify sourcebook code (such as, CE1) and first two words of title.

Mail orders for United States and Possessions, Australia, New Zealand, Canada, Latin America, and Japan to:
  Jossey-Bass Inc., Publishers
  433 California Street
  San Francisco, California 94104

Mail orders for all other parts of the world to:
  Jossey-Bass Limited
  28 Banner Street
  London EC1Y 8QE

New Directions for Continuing Education Series
Gordon G. Darkenwald, *Editor-in-Chief*
Alan B. Knox, *Consulting Editor*

CE1   *Enhancing Proficiencies of Continuing Educators,* Alan B. Knox
CE2   *Programming for Adults Facing Mid-Life Change,* Alan B. Knox
CE3   *Assessing the Impact of Continuing Education,* Alan B. Knox

CE4   *Attracting Able Instructors of Adults,* M. Alan Brown, Harlan G. Copeland
CE5   *Providing Continuing Education by Media and Technology,* Martin N. Chamberlain
CE6   *Teaching Adults Effectively,* Alan B. Knox
CE7   *Assessing Educational Needs of Adults,* Floyd C. Pennington
CE8   *Reaching Hard-to-Reach Adults,* Gordon G. Darkenwald, Gordon A. Larson
CE9   *Strengthening Internal Support for Continuing Education,* James C. Votruba
CE10 *Advising and Counseling Adult Learners,* Frank R. DiSilvestro
CE11 *Continuing Education for Community Leadership,* Harold W. Stubblefield
CE12 *Attracting External Funds for Continuing Education,* John H. Buskey
CE13 *Leadership Strategies for Meeting New Challenges,* Alan B. Knox
CE14 *Programs for Older Adults,* Morris A. Okun
CE15 *Linking Philosophy and Practice,* Sharan B. Merriam
CE16 *Creative Financing and Budgeting,* Travis Shipp
CE17 *Materials for Teaching Adults: Selection, Development, and Use,* John P. Wilson
CE18 *Strengthening Connections Between Education and Performance,* Stanley M. Grabowski
CE19 *Helping Adults Learn How to Learn,* Robert M. Smith
CE20 *Educational Outreach to Select Adult Populations,* Carol E. Kasworm
CE21 *Meeting Educational Needs of Young Adults,* Gordon G. Darkenwald, Alan B. Knox
CE22 *Designing and Implementing Effective Workshops,* Thomas J. Sork
CE23 *Realizing the Potential of Interorganizational Cooperation,* Hal Beder
CE24 *Evaluation for Program Improvement,* David Deshler
CE25 *Self-Directed Learning: From Theory to Practice,* Stephen Brookfield
CE26 *Involving Adults in the Educational Process,* Sandra H. Rosenblum
CE27 *Problems and Prospects in Continuing Professional Education,* Ronald M. Cervero, Craig L. Scanlan
CE28 *Improving Conference Design and Outcomes,* Paul J. Ilsley
CE29 *Personal Computers and the Adult Learner,* Barry Heermann
CE30 *Experiential and Simulation Techniques for Teaching Adults,* Linda H. Lewis
CE31 *Marketing Continuing Education,* Hal Beder
CE32 *Issues in Adult Career Counseling,* Juliet V. Miller, Mary Lynne Musgrove
CE33 *Responding to the Educational Needs of Today's Workplace,* Ivan Charner, Catherine A. Rolzinski

Contents

Editors' Notes 1
John A. Niemi, Dennis D. Gooler

1. Contexts of Using Technologies for Learning Outside the Classroom 3
John A. Niemi
Notes on the ongoing transformation of society through technological developments and other social and educational forces, and points out implications for using technologies for learning.

2. Utilizing Television 9
Peter Wiesner
Reports on the potential of television as a medium for learning outside the classroom, and emphasizes that its effectiveness depends on both the instructional design and support services that are organized when a program is finally shown.

3. Exploring the Educational Potential of Audio 19
Patricia A. Takemoto
Addresses the almost boundless educational potential of the audio media, focusing chiefly on radio and adding two other formats, tape recordings and teleconferencing.

4. Interactive Video: The Present and the Promise 29
Kerry A. Johnson
Investigates the potential of interactive video, raises issues that are being resolved, and presents selected exemplary programs that illustrate its uses.

5. Print Media 41
Michael G. Moore
Provides a review of print communication as a medium for distance education, stresses characteristics that course designers must take cognizance of, and underlines the importance of interaction between instructor and student that occurs through correspondence.

6. Computers in Adult Learning Outside the Classroom 51
Carol A. Carrier
Portrays use of computers in a variety of adult learning contexts and suggests some potentials and limitations of computers for learning in nonformal settings.

7. *Using Integrated Information Technologies for* 63
Out-of-Classroom Learning
Dennis D. Gooler

Explores potential benefits of using emerging integrated information technologies, and identifies policy issues raised by those technologies.

8. *Technology and Instructional Functions* 73
Daniel D. Pratt

Examines interactive and learner-centered use of technology in distance education through an exploration of three instructional functions: presenting content, monitoring progress, and providing feedback.

9. *Instructional Design and New Technologies* 89
Craig Locatis

Describes instructional designs and design guidelines for new information technologies used for adult learning in nonformal settings.

10. *Themes and Issues* 101
John A. Niemi, Dennis D. Gooler

Identifies major potential benefits of existing and emerging technologies for learning outside the classroom, and summarizes issues of concern to adult educators.

Index 109

Editors' Notes

Seven years have elapsed since *Providing Continuing Education by Media and Technology* was published as part of this series. The value of that sourcebook lay in its report on the possible uses of mass media to providers of continuing education. In a chapter predicting future uses of technology for learning, the authors acknowledged the importance of self-directed learning, but treated it within the narrow context of institutionally designed programs. This new sourcebook places emphasis not on education in the usual sense, but on nontraditional learning and on the learner. The authors of the various chapters bring to their task both research findings and a wealth of experience drawn from their involvement with adults engaged in learning.

In Chapter One, Niemi leads off with a discussion of the social and educational contexts of using technologies outside the classroom. In chapters two and three, Wiesner and Takemoto deal not only with television and radio, but also with other video and audio technologies, including cassettes. Johnson's chapter on interactive video, Chapter Four, puts him on the cutting edge along with the authors of chapters six and seven, Carrier and Gooler, who discuss computers and integrated information technologies. In Chapter Five, Moore stresses the enduring significance of the print media. The concerns of teachers and instructional designers are addressed by Pratt and Locatis in chapters eight and nine. Finally, in Chapter Ten, the editors synthesize and discuss the content of this sourcebook within a framework of six themes and issues central to the use of technologies for learning outside the classroom.

John A. Niemi
Dennis D. Gooler
Editors

John A. Niemi is professor of adult education, Northern Illinois University.

Dennis D. Gooler is professor of education, Northern Illinois University.

Many forces, including technology itself, have combined to free adults from the limitations of traditional learning.

Contexts of Using Technologies for Learning Outside the Classroom

John A. Niemi

The concept of learning outside the classroom is not new; libraries and institutions offering correspondence courses have played important roles in the education of adults since the nineteenth century. What is new is that the scope of this learning has been greatly extended due to a combination of major forces operating in U.S. society. The purpose of this chapter is to examine these forces, which form the social and educational contexts for using technologies for learning outside the classroom. The forces include technology itself, changing demographic data, altered career patterns and other life transitions, a shift in emphasis from education to learning, and a growing acceptance of the concept of lifelong learning.

The Long Shadow of Technology

It is no exaggeration to say that technology is casting a long shadow over the U.S. scene—to such an extent that the terms *information society* and *information age* are freely employed in everyday discourse. This transformation has resulted from dramatic technological development and the corresponding centrality of information in the personal and professional lives of many people. The situation represents a shift from the development of technologies that emphasize production to the development of technologies, notably computers and telecommunications, that help determine the very nature of the information society.

The social transformation that is occurring poses some important questions for society in general and for adult learners in particular. What can be done to prepare for life in a world undergoing constant transformation due to increasingly sophisticated technologies? How can those technologies and information-based systems be used to influence positively what and how learners learn, and with what consequences? The search is on for the answers.

Changing Demographic Data

It is no secret that the U.S. population is becoming old. According to the 1980 census, the lowest estimate of the adult population (eighteen years and over) was 175,286,000, in 1985 and will reach 196,205,000 by the year 2000. Of the 1985 total, 28,528,000, or approximately 16 percent, were sixty-five years or older and that category will grow to 33,621,000, or approximately 17 percent, in the year 2000. If the sixty-five years or older category were combined with the forty-five to sixty-four-year-old category, the total in 1985 would be 73,083,000, or approximately 41 percent of the total adult population, and will reach 93,480,000, or approximately 48 percent of the total adult population, in the year 2000 (U.S. Bureau of the Census, 1985).

The implications of this so-called "graying of America" for adult education are considerable. In the forty-five to sixty-four-year-old group, assistance with problems of career shifts and other life transitions is needed. In the sixty-five years and older group, the transition to retirement living creates a demand for continuing education in matters such as health, housing, money management, and leisure-time activities. The needs of women included in that group require special attention; the 1980 census estimated that they would outnumber men by 6,000,000 in 1985 and by 7,000,000 in the year 2000 (U.S. Bureau of the Census, 1985). To sum up, adult educators who have in the past devoted their energies to the concerns of young adults must now turn their attention to the concerns of the growing mass of middle-aged and older adults.

Altered Career Patterns and Other Life Transitions

For many years, middle age was considered to be a stable period of life, in which individuals enjoyed a settled occupation and from which they moved into retirement. During that period, other developmental tasks were linked to civic and social responsibilities and to family obligations.

For many of those individuals and for younger adults aged twenty-five and over, the situation has changed drastically, due in part to the impact of new technologies and the proliferation of knowledge. They have found themselves faced with a period of transition. As Aslanian and Brickell (1980, p. 66) reported, "most career transitions fell into one of three categories: (1) moving into a new job, (2) adapting to a changing job, and (3) advancing in a career." According to this study, 56 percent of those reporting on life transitions gave career as the reason for the pursuit of further learning. Another group was composed of dislocated workers who had lost their jobs because of automation, corporate mergers, and cutbacks. Unlike the previous group, these workers did not seek career changes voluntarily. Many of them were in need of retraining that would prepare them for new jobs.

Other life transitions are exemplified by women who resume their education, often after an extended period of not working, in order to prepare themselves for careers. In addition, transitions take place with respect to family, leisure, art, health, religion, and citizenship for all segments of society. According to Aslanian and Brickell (1980), family transitions emerge as the second most important category after careers. Such transitions include getting married, becoming pregnant, getting divorced, and moving to a new location. These life transitions, like altered career patterns, generate a need for programs to assist adults in solving their pressing problems.

Shift in Emphasis from Education to Learning

According to Moses (1971) and London and Wenkert (1974), a gradual shift occurred between 1940 and 1970, when a greater proportion of adult learners moved from participation in formal classroom learning to nontraditional, out-of-classroom learning. This nontraditional programming has been referred to by Wedemeyer (1981) as "learning at the back door," and includes distance learning, correspondence study, radio education, television education, satellite education, and self-directed learning.

The concept of self-directed learning has received widespread attention as the result of Tough's (1971) research on adult learning projects. The aim of self-directed learning is to move learners away from dependence on formal, structured approaches into situations in which they assume responsibility for their own learning. This requires a high degree of initiative, intelligence, and independence, as evidenced by Tough's (1971, p. 170) vision of the ideal self-directed learner: "The adult learner of the future will be highly competent in deciding what to learn, in planning and arranging his own learning. He will successfully diagnose and solve almost any problem or difficulty that arises. He will obtain appropriate help competently and quickly, but only when necessary."

Along with self-directed learning, much attention has been devoted in recent years to collaborative, or shared, learning. Here the learner and the teacher, whether on a one-to-one basis or in a classroom setting, have joint responsibility for the planning, conduct, and evaluation of learning experiences. The teacher's role is not to control learning, as in more structured settings, but to facilitate learning.

Another development has been a move away from nearly total preoccupation with the concerns of the providers of adult education toward the concerns of the learners they serve. Today there is an abundance of literature dealing with the special needs, interests, personalities, learning styles, and characteristics of learners. The characteristics include the wide range of roles that adults play, the wealth of life experience that they bring to learning, their often superior motivation, and, on the negative side, the anxieties they frequently suffer in facing both the demands imposed on them by new learning and the restrictions of the aging process. As the above discussion indicates, the shift in emphasis from education to learning has cast the adult learner in an increasingly active role in which he or she can operate effectively both in a traditional classroom setting and independently outside the classroom.

Lifelong Learning

The concept of lifelong learning grew in importance in the 1970s with the realization that the notion that one's education is finished on completion of a certain period of formal schooling belonged to an era of relative stability in society and was inappropriate for a society undergoing sweeping changes in its values, attitudes, and institutions. Moreover, adults are now living longer, as the demographic data indicate, and they are enjoying higher levels of education. "Lifelong education" was the term used by UNESCO in 1972, and again in 1985, when an important concept, the right to learn, was added. Seen as a fundamental right and a requisite for human development, the right to learn was described by UNESCO (1985, p. 67) as follows: "The right to read and write; to question and analyze; the right to imagine and create; the right to read [about] one's own world and to write history; the right to have access to educational resources; the right to develop individual and collective skills."

Teachers and program designers need to embrace the concept of lifelong learning in order to keep abreast of new knowledge and skills to enhance their own proficiency. In so doing they act as role models who can imbue learners with an appreciation of lifelong learning. Thus learners will come to realize that there is an ever-widening pool of knowledge, skills, and attitudes to help them adapt to the inexorable changes in their life patterns.

Implications for Using Technologies Outside the Classroom

The forces and developments outlined above suggest some practical implications for the uses of technologies in learning outside the classroom. For example, the demographic data show that the U.S. population is getting older, and so the question arises: As middle-aged and older adults strive to cope with problems peculiar to their age groups, how can technologies assist their learning? An important point to remember is that, unlike young adults whose exposure to technologies began early in life and who are therefore comfortable with them, older adults regard many technologies—especially advanced ones—with suspicion and, in some cases, fear that borders on phobia. Yet these same technologies can satisfy the learning needs of many older adults, especially those who lead isolated lives in their retirement years for reasons associated with health, fear of crime, or geographic location. In planning for the learning needs of middle-aged and older adults, program designers and teachers must understand the need to allay learners' anxieties about technologies used for learning outside the classroom.

In using technologies to assist adults with altered career patterns and other life transitions, program designers and teachers should bear in mind that they are dealing with many special groups—dislocated workers, women entering or returning to the workforce, and professionals who are committed to advancing their careers—as well as those experiencing other life transitions such as the poor, the disabled, the incarcerated, the divorced, and so on. In practical terms, this means that program designers and teachers should remember that each group has distinctive characteristics, interests, needs, and motivations, and should plan systematically to assess these elements in planning programs. Otherwise, program designers and teachers run the risk of creating "top down" programs, which often fail because the participants view them as irrelevant or of little help in solving practical problems. Many of the technologies described in this volume are particularly capable of delivering instruction outside the classroom to meet the unique needs of adult learners.

In the shift of emphasis from education to learning, there are also implications for program designers, teachers, and learners who are using technologies for learning outside the classroom. Program designers must have a thorough grasp of the capabilities of the various technologies, of ways in which to integrate them, and of ways in which to promote interactivity with learners.

Teachers also require this knowledge. In addition, they have the tasks of familiarizing learners with new technologies, helping learners to choose technologies appropriate both to their own learning styles and to the content, and, finally, lending support and encouragement to learners in their search for new knowledge.

Learners must also understand the capabilities of various technologies if they are to move toward self-direction in learning outside the classroom. Moreover, they must learn how to adapt technologies to their own learning styles and how to select wisely, from the available technologies, those that will help produce solutions to particular problems.

Perhaps technology will cast its longest shadow on the growing importance of learning as a lifelong process. But, in order for learners to exploit the full potential of technology for individual and societal advancement, it is essential for society to initiate policies that deal with access and equity on behalf of all citizens—not just a favored few—as they exercise their right to learn. Access and equity must extend to technologies used outside the classroom.

If those principles are observed, and if adults are assisted in making judicious choices of technologies that will further their learning, it may be possible to translate the rhetoric of lifelong learning into action.

References

Aslanian, C. B., and Brickell, H. M. *Americans in Transition: Life Changes as Reasons for Adult Learning.* New York: College Entrance Examination Board, 1980.

London, J., and Wenkert, R. "Adult Education: Definition, Description, and Analysis." In D. W. Swift (ed.), *American Education: Definition, Description, and Analysis.* Boston, Mass.: Houghton Mifflin, 1974.

Moses, S. *Learning Force: A More Comprehensive Framework for Educational Policy.* Syracuse, N.Y.: Syracuse University Publications in Continuing Education, 1971.

Tough, A. *The Adult's Learning Projects: A Fresh Approach to Theory and Practice in Adult Learning.* Toronto: OISE, 1971.

UNESCO. *Fourth International Conference on Adult Education: Final Report.* Paris: UNESCO, 1985.

U.S. Bureau of the Census. *Statistical Abstract of the United States: 1986.* (106th ed.) Washington, D.C.: U.S. Bureau of the Census, 1985.

Wedemeyer, C. A. *Learning at the Back Door: Reflections on NonTraditional Learning in the Lifespan.* Madison: University of Wisconsin Press, 1981.

John A. Niemi is professor of adult education at Northern Illinois University. He was a Fulbright professor of adult education at the University of Helsinki. He is chair of the Commission of Professors of Adult Education.

Television is a powerful medium for reaching learners outside the classroom; however, lack of contact is a major limitation in its application.

Utilizing Television

Peter Wiesner

Although television is a major source of information and entertainment, there are both benefits and pitfalls in its use as an educational medium. Some writers, including Hawkridge (1983) and Purdie (1978), underscore its value in reaching learners outside of traditional classroom settings. Others caution that television by itself is not a satisfactory replacement for traditional face-to-face instruction.

According to Orndorff (1976), television cannot replace talented teachers, even though it is an effective tool for reaching individual learners. Harrington (1977) notes that many students drop out of television courses because of the lack of personal contact. Schramm (1981) wonders whether television encourages a taste for information rather than knowledge.

Television is technically capable of being a substitute for the classroom experience. By doing so, it displaces the social dimension of the teaching but also makes educational services accessible to those who cannot avail themselves of traditional schooling. Educational services can be expanded and enhanced through television. The problem is defining television's proper role and use outside the classroom.

Broadcast Television

As a mass medium, television informs, persuades, entertains, and occasionally instructs. The economics of broadcasting require the attraction of large audiences; for this reason, instructional programs are less likely to be included in a schedule if they lack popular appeal. However, instructional programs, such as "The French Chef," a cooking series by Julia Child, have attracted a general viewership during prime time.

Although broadcast television stations in commercial markets place low priority on direct instruction, they nonetheless provide nonformal educational resources for viewers through documentaries, news programs, talk shows, cultural specials, and public affairs programs. Instruction is provided by the college-credit telecourses offered by the Public Broadcasting Service (PBS) in cooperation with local colleges and universities. Many of these, such as "Shakespeare," "The Art of Being Human," "Understanding Human Behavior," "Earth, Sea, and Sky," and "Vietnam: A Television History" are of general interest and appeal.

Narrowcast Television

Local cable access and the increased number of channels available via satellite as well as microwave transmission permit the "narrowcasting" of educational and instructional programs that otherwise would not be shown on broadcast stations. For example, the Association for Media-Based Continuing Education for Engineers (AMCEE) in Atlanta, Georgia, with a membership of more than thirty universities, offers short telecourses on its own satellite network. The National University Teleconference Network (NUTN), a consortium of more than 150 universities headquartered at Oklahoma State University, transmits satellite teleconferences on topics such as world food day, corporate culture, biodiversity, and science and technology. Satellite Communication for Learning Associated (SCOLA) at Creighton University in Omaha, Nebraska, is a pioneer in importing foreign programming (redistributed via domestic satellites) for use in university language programs.

Many universities, such as Boston, California State at Sacramento, Maryland, Stanford, and George Washington, are transmitting video through Instructional Television Fixed Service (ITFS), a microwave frequency that requires a special antenna for reception. In some states, such as Indiana and Texas, microwave and ITFS networks permit video programming to be transmitted by universities from one part of a state to another.

Many colleges and universities offer telecourses and other programs on local cable access channels. Pennsylvania State University has developed a statewide cable network used for relaying telecourses, teleconferences, and other educational programming. In New Jersey, the Cable Television Network, a statewide cable network owned by cable operators, makes time available to colleges and universities during non-prime-time hours.

Nonbroadcast Cassette Distribution

Videocassettes have become commonplace in industry, schools, libraries, and the home. According to Brush and Brush (1986), some 8,500 companies and other organizations spent at least $2.3 billion in 1985 on producing videos for training, communication, and promotion. There is also a growing market for home video. Consumers can purchase entertainment and educational cassettes by mail for not much more than the price of a hardcover book.

According to Brown (1985), 19 percent of all homes have a videocassette recorder, and by 1990 that number will rise to 30 percent. There are thousands of retail video outlets and numerous mail-order sources for video rental and purchase. Although now used primarily for entertainment, videocassettes will become, as audiocasettes already are, a major source for home-based instruction, including exercise programs, language instruction, real estate, and career development. Increasingly, public libraries are stimulating the educational use of home video by carrying titles on VHS, beta, and 8 mm for general circulation.

Utilization of Television Outside the Classroom

The desirability of television outside the classroom depends on cost, availability of programming, and access to the means of producing and disseminating video.

In distance education, educators weigh the cost-effectiveness and feasibility of television against radio, telephone, computers, correspondence by mail, face-to-face instruction, or a combination of all of these. When television primarily extends the classroom through telecommunications, as in many courses taught live via satellite and ITFS, the creative use of this medium is likely to be of secondary importance. This can happen when television is used simply to transmit lecture-demonstrations.

When educators wish to unleash the creative powers of the television medium through documentary, dramatization, and graphics techniques, they must weigh the costs of acquiring already-produced programs, such as telecourses, against the cost of producing their own. They may even combine the "talking head" variety of television—characterized by the predominant use of tight shots of on-camera talent without support visuals—with high-quality prerecorded programs and segments. Original production can cost more than $2,000 per minute; for this reason, educators are likely to begin with a search for prerecorded materials relevant to the curriculum.

The decision to produce or acquire video is generally affected by the availability and cost of telecommunications systems, including commercial and public broadcast stations as well as ITFS, satellite, and cable narrowcast channels. Often, colleges and other adult education organizations join consortia to share the cost of offering live and prerecorded materials.

Educational institutions also have the option of making videocassettes available outside the classroom through learning centers and libraries, and they can choose among more than 1,100 video courses beyond high school produced by over 200 colleges, universities, businesses, and broadcasters. Although cassettes could be mailed directly to students with access to videocassette recorders, the costs of video duplication, software rights, mailing, and handling may be excessive.

Although television is widely used, not all educators embrace mediated instruction because, according to Evans (1968), they fear that television and other telecommunications media, used as the primary source of instruction, will denigrate the role of the teacher. Many doubt that television can match the quality of a classroom discussion or the responsibility exercised by a teacher in keeping the teaching-learning process current and relevant to society and the learner. They suspect that noninteractive television viewing encourages passivity.

Noting the limitations of noninteractive television, Lentz (1982, p. 325) states that "spoken language in face-to-face contact . . . is the most accurate method of testing the truth of our knowledge of the world." Wedemeyer and Childs (1961) stress that television should provide for two-way communication and that it should maintain the centrality of the individual and allow for preplanned learning not merely passive watching and listening. Another writer, Perrin (1973), observes that television is best used when it is an integral component with other methods, techniques, and media in a total learning system.

The fact that television has often been used as a stop-gap measure when there is a teacher or facilities shortage does not enhance its status among educators. There is a tendency to regard it as a second-best way to deliver instructional services to people in marginal situations outside the classroom. Yet television's strong point is making education possible in marginal situations. Satellite transmissions can bring formal courses to students in remote areas, as the program "Learn Alaska," produced under the auspices of the University of Alaska and other state agencies, did to Eskimo villages in Alaska. Telecourses on public television and cable increase access to schooling for homemakers, the employed, and the handicapped; such courses provide a feasible way for out-of-school adults to pursue lifelong learning goals.

In recent years, television gained a modicum of acceptability in education, perhaps because of the legacy of research indicating its worth, which is comparable to face-to-face instruction. Most studies indicate that television can match classroom-based instruction in terms of measurable learning outcomes and student attitudes. There is no lack of documentation and promotion of television, as reflected in publications by Coastline Community College, University of Maryland, and other organizations engaged in producing and distributing telecourses.

Still, when it comes to documenting the experience of distance learners, the research on television falls short. According to Holmberg (1977) and Walshok (1980), much of the research comparing television to face-to-face instruction has not addressed the role of interpersonal contact in television-based educational programs. However, many writers have recognized that television can affect the role of teachers and how they interact with learners. For example, Hawkridge (1983, p. 156) notes that new instructional technology creates a situation that puts "students in control and asks new roles of teachers as technicians, selectors of courseware, individualizers of instruction, managers, schedulers, and advisers."

The meager contact between telecourse students and their instructors has been documented in a study by Wiesner (1986), who found that students who need to earn credits without having to attend class are willing to sacrifice contact for the sake of convenience. Some may even prefer the anonymity of learning outside the classroom. From an educator's point of view, the question is to what extent the convenience of telecourse justifies the lack of interaction and contact. For example, when prerecorded videos replace the live lecture, as they do in many telecourses, materials may become dated without being adequately scrutinized by the instructor and students through normal class discussion. The question then becomes, who will take on the responsibility for authenticating course content when technology, not teachers, provides the direct link with students?

Television in Adult Education

Mass media, mostly radio and some television, has increased the accessibility of adult education throughout the world (Bates, 1984). However, costs of television production, transmission, and reception have limited the educational use of television broadcasts in developing countries, especially in rural areas. In developed countries, television has been used in a marginal way to extend high school and university-level courses to the home.

In the United States, many television courses have dealt with practical adult education topics, such as gardening, personal finance, child development, consumer education, and career development. Community college noncredit, as well as credit, telecourses also expose adults to the arts, sciences, social sciences, and humanities.

"Operation Alphabet" was one of the first attempts to use television to reach nonreaders who were not enrolled in traditional adult basic education programs. This series, produced by WPVI-TV in Philadelphia in the 1960s, was quintessential talking head television, which characterized much of early instructional television. Broadcast television programs were also developed for high school equivalency (GED) diplomas. "Your Future Is Now," produced by the New York Manpower Institute, was accompanied by workbooks. Kentucky Educational Television (KET) produced a GED series with high production values, including documentary segments and dramatizations that reached adult learners through broadcasts and videotape playback in adult learning centers. There were also scattered efforts to use television in teaching English as a second language to nonspeakers.

In the 1980s television programs relevant to adult basic education continue to be produced for broadcast and nonbroadcast distribution. Recently, "Project Plus," undertaken jointly by PBS and ABC, used television to raise public awareness about illiteracy. WXYZ in Detroit produced the thirty-program series "Learn to Read" for broadcast. Kentucky education television produced "Another Page," an adult reading series aimed at the sixth-grade level, and also "GED on TV" to replace the earlier KET GED series, which was used nationally in high school equivalency programs.

Instructional television in adult basic education has been more successful in presenting informational and motivational topics than literacy skills training. One reason is that although television can convey discrete information, such as vocabulary and grammatical concepts, it is limited in teaching interactive skills such as connected reading. However, television has proved to be an effective medium for consumer education, life skills, and job readiness, and series on these topics have been produced by the University of Wisconsin, Maryland Public Broadcasting, Mississippi Educational Television, and others for both broadcast and learning center use.

The success of educational radio and television with disadvantaged adults depends, in large part, on proper instructional design not only of the television programs themselves but also of the support systems for the programs' effective utilization. If television is to be used effectively, planning must take into account not only learning theory and media design principles but also psychological and cultural factors that influence participation in education. Close attention should be paid to the development of a viewer support system that will motivate adults to sustain participation. For example, in literacy training, television can be usefully employed in conjunction with tutoring and class sessions. In this context, prerecorded television programs can be effective in presenting a standard curriculum and in helping pace and motivate learning; however, without viewer support such as discussion groups, motivation and participation tend to drop off.

To sustain involvement in television-based lessons, educators in developing countries organized listening and viewing groups that not only made cost-effective use of receivers but also provided a social context for learning to take place. The importance of viewer support services was realized in adult basic education television projects, including literacy training, in developing countries such as Colombia, India, and Niger.

One such project was the Satellite Instructional Television Experiment (SITE), a one-year experiment during the mid 1970s that brought educational programming to children and adults in remote villages in India. According to Agraval (1984), the major lesson learned from SITE is that software planning requires more time than hardware development and that it must take into account local economic and cultural factors. Television thus offers no panacea for reaching nonreaders and other disadvantaged adults who need personal attention in a familiar setting to bolster confidence. Certainly, one-way television broadcasts do not provide the desirable level of interactivity found in a classroom. However, when used as an audiovisual aid in support of adult basic education, television can serve a valuable function in visualizing and dramatizing concepts.

Television in Higher Education

In higher education, television has long been a tool in extension and distance education. According to Saettler (1968), the first instructional use of television in higher education was provided by the State University of Iowa between 1932 and 1938. In 1951 Western Reserve University offered the first credit-bearing courses on television. In 1956 the Chicago TV College undertook the first large-scale effort to offer open-circuit televised courses for college credit to adults unable to attend on-campus courses. And in the fifties and sixties, many colleges employed closed-circuit television to meet the rising demand for higher education during a time of teacher and classroom shortages.

Television also met the growing demand for higher education abroad. Courses were offered on television in Germany, Israel, Italy, Poland, the Soviet Union, the People's Republic of China, and other countries. In Great Britain, the Open University provided a model for using television in conjunction with other administrative structures and thus made higher education accessible to nontraditional adult students.

Instructional broadcasts in higher education included live and recorded lectures as well as programs that used production techniques familiar to the general television viewer. Telecourses, as such, began to add production values to lecture-demonstrations that in earlier years defined instructional television. For example, telecourses such as "Ascent of Man" and "The Growing Years" made extensive use of documentary techniques and graphics to enhance verbal information. The talking head approach to instructional television thus fell out of fashion as telecourse producers with ample production budgets developed programs that would not only attract credit-seeking students but also a sufficiently large general interest audience to justify the use of broadcast time.

Anticipating a decline in college enrollments in the seventies and eighties, both community and four-year colleges used open-circuit television to reach new students, especially working adults and homemakers unable to attend on-campus courses. The production and distribution of telecourses were facilitated through regional and national consortia of two-year and four-year colleges. Studies and reports promoted telecourses during the growth era of the seventies, and in 1982 Walter Annenberg, former ambassador to Great Britain, funded the development of telecourses to be used in a national "College of the Air." At about that time, the Corporation for Public Broadcasting instituted PTV-3, the Adult Learning Service, which by 1986 offered a total of twenty-eight courses in the arts and humanities, business and technology, history, professional development and teacher education, science and health, and social sciences.

According to a survey by Munshi (1979), more than 600 colleges and universities offered telecourses for credit in 1979. Another survey by the Corporation for Public Broadcasting (1986) accounted for 10,500 telecourses offered in 1985 by more than 900, or 32 percent, of U.S. two-year and four-year institutions. The total national course enrollment was nearly 400,000, with an average of thirty-eight students per course. Most telecourses were shown over a fifteen-week period at the rate of one or two programs per week, corresponding to the traditional college semester, although some, offered through the National University Consortium, involved fewer television programs and relied heavily on print materials.

In a typical telecourse, a study guide coordinates television programs, textbook, and other assignments so that minimal guidance of distance learners is required. These study guides usually contain information about course procedures and the objectives and study plan for each week or unit. Administrative guides refer teachers to learning resources and also suggest ways of using correspondence, telephone conversations, and seminars for establishing and maintaining contact.

Although telecourses standardize the presentation of content through television, the instructor at a given institution is free to set standards and procedures for the course. Grades may be based on proctored exams, papers, and other projects. Some instructors place little emphasis on the content presented in the television programs. Others require students to master the content presented on television as well as in the readings.

Not only is there variation in the role of television in telecourses but the amount of personal contact that students have with their instructors and fellow students also varies. At some institutions, students are required to attend orientation and seminar sessions. At others, however, telecourses are simply old-fashioned correspondence courses that are televised, which allow little contact with an instructor.

Still, for many distance learners, the option to learn via television outweighs its inherent limitation of contact with the instructor and fellow students. One major advantage of television is that it is a convenient, flexible option for those who cannot afford the time and cost of traveling to class. The extent to which television realizes its potential as an educational resource depends not only on appropriate instructional design and production values but on the way support services are organized when the programs are finally shown.

The Future

Television is becoming increasingly integrated with other telecommunications media. Voice, data, and video—already carried simultaneously via satellite, coaxial cable, and land lines—are also being brought together at the user level through personal computers, videodisc, *cd rom,* teletext, and videotext. Technological advances, such as video compression, will increase the potential video traffic by reducing the band width required for transmission.

Television as a one-way educational medium on broadcast stations will continue to respond to general audience needs. Cable television and direct broadcast satellite reception for both institutional and consumer markets have already opened up channels for instructional narrowcasting, and the problem will be to generate sufficient income to enable producing agencies to sustain production.

As the use of telecommunications media at the consumer level grows and the production and transmission cost becomes lower, it is likely that the per unit costs of a given television program will be reduced in an expanding institutional and home video market. In industry, interactive as well as one-way video will continue to dominate corporate communication and training. In education, colleges and universities will expand the use of video to extend continuing and graduate education. With the expected shortage of college teachers in the nineties, video and other technologies are likely to be used to provide services to traditional as well as nontraditional college students. In many cases, video will be used for live interactive presentations as well as prerecorded telecourses.

In the coming decades, television will continue to play an important part in extending education beyond the classroom. Therefore, educators will have to confront the issue of cost-effectiveness and struggle to balance media production values with academic requirements for accuracy, relevance, and currency.

Equally important, educators will have to face the challenge of using television—with all of its advantages and limitations—without depersonalizing the teaching-learning process.

References

Agraval, B. C. "Satellite Instructional Television: SITE in India." In G. Gerbner and M. Siefert (eds.), *World Communications: A Handbook.* New York: Longman, 1984.

Bates, A. W. "Broadcast Television in Distance Education." In A. W. Bates (ed.), *The Role of Technology in Distance Education*. New York: St. Martin's Press, 1984.

Brown, L. *Channels of Communication, the Essential 1985 Field Guide to the Electronic Media: Revolution at the Hearth*. New York: Media Commentary Council, 1985.

Brush, J., and Brush, D. *Private Television Communications: The New Directions*. (The Fourth Brush Report.) Cold Spring, N.Y.: HI Press, 1986.

Corporation for Public Broadcasting. "A National Study of the Educational Uses of Telecommunications Technology in America's Colleges and Universities." *Research Notes*, 1986, *21*, 1–14.

Evans, R. E. *Resistance to Innovation in Higher Education: A Social-Psychological Exploration Focused on Television and the Establishment*. San Francisco: Jossey-Bass, 1968.

Harrington, H. "New Opportunities: Off-Campus Credits." In F. H. Harrington (ed.), *The Future of Adult Education*. San Francisco: Jossey-Bass, 1977.

Hawkridge, D. *New Information Technology in Education*. Baltimore, Md.: Johns Hopkins University Press, 1983.

Holmberg, B. *Distance Education: A Survey and Bibliography*. New York: Nichols, 1977.

Lentz, T. M. "The Medium Is the Madness: Television and the Pseudo-Oral Tradition in America's Future." In H. F. Didsbury, Jr. (ed.), *Communications and the Future: Prospects, Promise, and Problems*. Bethesda, Md.: World Future Society, 1982.

Munshi, K. S. *Telecourses: Reflections '79; Station-College Executive Project in Adult Learning*. Washington, D.C.: Corporation for Public Broadcasting, 1979.

Orndorff, J. E. *Project Reach: Final Report*. Washington, D.C.: Fund for the Improvement of Postsecondary Education, U.S. Dept. of Education, 1976. (ED 148 377)

Perrin, D. G. "Synopsis of Educational Television." In J. Ackerman and J. Lipsitz (eds.), *Instructional Television*. Englewood Cliffs, N.J.: Instructional Technology, 1973.

Purdie, L. "Telecourse Students: How Well Do They Learn?" Paper presented at annual AAJCA meeting in Atlanta, April 1978. (ED 158 851)

Saettler, P. *A History of Instructional Technology*. New York: McGraw-Hill, 1968.

Schramm, W. *Mass Communication Yearbook*. Vol. 2. Newbury Park, Calif.: Sage, 1981.

Walshok, M. L. "Some Unanswered Questions About Telecommunication and Adult Learning." In M. N. Chamberlain (ed.), *Providing Continuing Education by Media and Technology*. New Directions for Continuing Education, no. 5. San Francisco: Jossey-Bass, 1980.

Wedemeyer, C. A., and Childs, G. B. *New Perspectives in University Correspondence Study*. Chicago: Center for the Study of Liberal Education for Adults, 1961.

Wiesner, P. "Communication in Distance Learning: An Exploratory Field Study of Adults Enrolled in Telecourses Offered by New Jersey Community College Students." Unpublished dissertation, Rutgers University, 1986.

Peter Wiesner is coordinator of academic television, Rutgers University, New Brunswick, New Jersey.

From jogging while listening to a lecture on Jacksonian democracy to studying Sartre in the shower, new technological developments in the audio medium have altered the definition of the classroom.

Exploring the Educational Potential of Audio

Patricia A. Takemoto

"More learning and teaching go on throughout life outside the classroom than in," wrote Charles Wedemeyer (1981, p. 30). With each passing year, that insightful statement rings louder and truer. As technological developments rapidly expand in all forms of electronic media, and specificially in audio, today's classroom can literally be almost anywhere—at the industrial worksite interconnected via audio teleconference equipment; in an automobile equipped with a radio or audiocassette deck; at home with listeners by a radio, audiocassette player, compact disc player, or telephone; even in the shower with a waterproof radio! Quite feasibly, with the help of the audio medium, there is no place that is "outside the classroom" anymore.

This chapter addresses the virtually boundless educational potential of the audio media; while this chapter focuses primarily on radio, two other audio formats with great educational applications—tape recordings (records, cassettes, discs, reel-to-reel tapes) and teleconferencing—are also discussed. One of the main benefits that the versatility of the audio media brings to education is the ability to extend learning opportunities to a far greater audience than the formal student. Learning occurs not only in what Houle (1972) calls planned activities "by design," but by chance as well, in situations that Little (1979) identified as "fortuitous and unintentional" and Reischmann (1986) characterizes as "en passant." It is especially in these informal learning situations that the power of mass media and its ability to provide information quickly, efficiently, and effectively to great numbers of people is clearly evident.

Benefits of Audio Technology

Compared to other electronic communications media, audio, and especially radio, has the educational advantages of being inexpensive, ubiquitous, easy to operate, and portable. Other forms of mediated technology often involve expensive and sometimes complex hardware and software designed for what Ross (1982-83) calls the "information elite," those who can afford such equipment and the accompanying software. The audio medium, on the other hand, provides the listener, whether a learner by chance or by design, with wide-ranging and usually low-cost access to a plethora of programs and information. Broadcast radio's forte, especially with satellite and cable delivery systems, lies in its ability to reach greater audiences inexpensively and conveniently.

Such accessibility to course-specific programs enables the mass audience of chance learners and casual listeners to participate along with the deliberate, intentional, and directed students. Thus, not only are the categories of learners expanded, but the distinctions are blurred between learning, which Little (1979) defines as a natural and psychological process of gaining or changing insights, and education, the more deliberate and systematic effort to transmit or to acquire specific knowledge. While one might learn from any life experience, such as random radio broadcasts, conversations, informal readings, television programs, and so on, one is educated by systematically undertaking deliberate learning activities. The richness of the audio medium allows for the same material to serve both these learning contexts, and Durbridge (1984) identifies some basic characteristics that all forms of audio share:

1. Voices can convey enthusiasm for subject matter and provide audible cues and clarity about the meaning of words and about speakers themselves, thus breaking down some barriers and giving a sense of the teacher as a human being.
2. Listening can occur while the hands and eyes are free to do other things, either relevant learning activity (reading music scores, studying maps or paintings) or quite unrelated activity (driving a car, ironing, jogging).
3. Audio can convey certain kinds of abstract information more quickly than the print medium.
4. Audio relays information over time, unlike print, where the information is on constant display. In a question-and-answer situation, the audio format may more effectively prolong interest and build suspense.

5. Students seem to comply more readily with instruction when they hear it than when they read it.

Obviously, a listener may have several goals and therefore may gain multiple results. But if something more than casual learning is to occur, the following factors will play an important part in determining which specific audio medium would be the most effective and appropriate:

- Accessibility to the audio materials, either via broadcast or hard copy
- Quality and appropriateness of the audio treatment to the subject matter
- Integration of the learning materials (the texts, programs, and examinations) so that the listener can understand the relationship among these components and know how to use them in the learning process
- Control of the pace at which the listener hears and absorbs the material for review, analysis, and reflection
- Interactivity between and among instructor, students, and the material.

Differentiation Among Audio Technologies

Radio, audio recordings, and teleconferencing differ mainly in the amount of control and interactivity each format affords the learner.

Radio. Bates and Kern (1977, p. 3) describe radio as a "transient, immediate, and continuous medium"—transient because the program is usually broadcast only once, immediate because the broadcasts are received by the listener as soon as they are transmitted, and continuous because the programs continue on, regardless of whether the listener turns the radio off or wishes to have some material repeated. Because of these characteristics, there are some types of material and educational uses that are more appropriate than others for radio. The British Open University, a pioneer in mediated distance learning, has sponsored a great deal of research on radio and audiocassette instruction. Bates (1979, p. 4) identifies the following contexts in which radio is particularly well suited for formal education:

1. When relating the principles and concepts of the course material to current events (for example, news stories and recent social, environmental, and political developments);
2. When updating course materials to take account of events occurring during the life of the course;
3. When providing external criticism or alternative viewpoints to the already-prepared course material; and
4. In circumstances where only one broadcast transmission of the material would generally be considered sufficient, such as:
    - An introduction, summary, or overview of a unit

- A discussion where the raising of issues and counter-views is considered to be more important than the actual arguments themselves
- When an experience—such as a performance of music, a dramatization, or a poetry reading—is considered to be of more value than an intellectual analysis of concepts or the provision of information
- A single argument or story where analysis is less important than familiarizing the student with the material.

Radio has other irrefutable educational advantages. It is the most cost-effective means of mass instruction to large groups of learners. It is the easiest way to reach wide audiences of potential learners and to pace the study and sustain the motivation of current students. Radio's approach can be relevant, current, local, and personal. If a radio program has a telephone call-in feature, a degree of interactivity can be designed into the course whereby the instructors and students/listeners can discuss and share aspects of the program with a mass audience of other listeners. In the United States, because of National Public Radio's ability to acquire one-time broadcast rights to most material for educational purposes, copyright restrictions are often less stringent for radio than for cassette or other recorded versions of the material, especially if the recordings are to be sold.

However, radio has some serious limitations, especially for formal education. Because of the expense of producing broadcast-quality material and the cost of studio and tower transmissions, radio is only cost-effective when the intent is to reach large numbers of listeners. The scarcity of prime air time has always been a great problem in broadcasting; and as the number of broadcast courses increases, so does the competition for what the British Open University calls convenient, "sociable air time." The need for repeat broadcasts complicates the scheduling problems further; unless students are able to obtain tape recordings of the programs, they have virtually no opportunity to review the material in depth and at their own pace and thus have very little control of the material. The increasing use of sideband radio frequency services (Subsidiary Communications Authorization or SCA) broadcasts provides a possible solution to the scheduling problem because it allows a radio station to transmit programs to specialized audiences over alternative FM frequencies. But stations need SCA transmitters, and listeners need special receivers, both of which increase costs and decrease accessibility.

There are often serious philosophical differences between the priorities of the educator, the producer, and the broadcaster, each of whom may have different agendas and standards of judgment of production value. For broadcast purposes, radio producers often feel that they must compete in terms of dynamism, personality, and lively pace with other on-air programs. But faster pacing can result in incomprehensible (and boring) programs that are too densely packed with information, facts, and reiteration. Sometimes radio's ability to reach large numbers of people may create the impression that these courses are more formal and the instructor more intimidating than would be the case in a classroom situation. Thus the educator, broadcaster, and producer must walk the fine line between style and substance; this often causes policy dilemmas that are rarely solved to everyone's satisfaction unless a single entity (like the British Open University) can control all aspects of the course design, production, and broadcast schedule.

In summary, the radio generally provides the greatest mass access to educational materials, and radio programs can, if designed properly, very effectively communicate certain types of information within certain learning contexts. Its upbeat, fast-paced format can be popular, timely, and appealing. Its programs are generally effective for informal learners and the general public and can provide background information for formal students. But for conveying detailed analyses, complex arguments, or numerous examples and facts, other audio formats or print are probably more effective. The growing trend is to use radio more selectively for what it can do best: highlight and publicize courses to mass audiences.

Although other nonbroadcast media may sometimes be better suited for actual instructional activities, there are some exciting educational ventures being conveyed via radio. More formal educational radio activity occurs below the postsecondary level, especially with stations licensed to the community or to local or state educational boards. For example, KBPS in Portland, Oregon, like many other stations with an established presence in the educational community, serves the elementary and middle school districts with citywide AM broadcasts of student-produced radio dramas, student panel discussions, "spell-downs," and math "solve-it" programs. Portland high school students have the opportunity to acquire production and engineering training by writing, producing, and staffing "19 Magazine," a weekly program directed to teenage listeners. Similarly, WBEZ in Chicago, Illinois, licensed to the Chicago Board of Education, produces "Airplay" magazine, with features of book reviews, drama, comedy, and career planning advice directed to the high school audience. These programs are broadcast during the daytime hours, sometimes with options for obtaining tape recordings for later listening.

At the higher educational level, the use of radio is more modest, in part because the complexity of information conveyed in college-level courses is often not well suited for radio and in part because there are fewer college-age listeners than elementary and secondary school-age listeners. Radio at the higher education level is most often used to augment courses that are most amenable to audio, such as foreign language instruction, technical terminology courses, and music appreciation. Riccobono

(1986) reports that even in these cases, the material is also likely to be available via tape recordings in language laboratories and listening rooms.

Stations like WDCB, licensed to the College of DuPage in Illinois, with a clear mission to support instruction to nontraditional students, may broadcast some of their courses because they serve a large enrollment of working adults and part-time, off-campus students. However, most public radio stations fulfill their FCC-mandated commitments with more generalized news, information, and cultural/public affairs programming. WHA-Radio in Madison, Wisconsin, is unique in its coproduction, with the University of Wisconsin, of a series of credit-bearing radio courses called the "University of the Air." These semester-long courses are comprised of weekly statewide radio broadcasts (a lecture and telephone call-in format), combined with reading and written assignments and proctored examinations. The openness of radio broadcasts makes these courses, lectures, and discussions accessible to the casual listener as well as the enrolled student. However, such programs are rare, since public radio stations, needing to broaden their financial base by increasing their listenership, must strive to serve a broader audience.

One promising development is that with the increasing utilization of the sideband radio service (SCA) mentioned earlier and cable delivery systems, more specialized listening audiences—such as the visually handicapped, the homebound, the multicultural listener, the distant learner, and those engaged in professional training—are beginning to be better served. While the primary channel of WOSU in Columbus, Ohio, broadcasts classical music, a subsidiary channel makes French and German language instruction available to college students at Ohio State University. Anchorage Community College broadcasts an audio course to its geographically isolated students over a TV cable channel and uses the video portion to provide information on course registration and to make other course-related announcements. Thus, although often regarded as the missed opportunity and the forgotten medium, radio has played a relatively quiet but steady role in U.S. formal education.

Audio Recordings. With the exciting technological developments in the area of audio recording—especially with audiocassettes, compact discs, and the availability of inexpensive, portable playback equipment—the potential for audio-based instruction has blossomed in the past decade. Compared to radio, Bates and Kern (1977, p. 2) call audio recordings a "permanent, time-free interruptable medium"—permanent because the audio material is stored in hard copy form, time-free because it is not tied to a broadcast schedule, and interruptable because the listener can stop the recording at any point, come back to it later, replay portions of previous material, or move ahead to new material. This element of greater control of audio material has made this medium, especially in the audiocassette format, an extremely attractive educational tool. The advantage that the cassette has over other forms of recordings—records, reel-to-reel tapes, and compact discs—are several. Cassette playback and recording equipment is now readily available in small, lightweight, portable, easy-to-operate, and inexpensive models; it is also almost as ubiquitous as the radio. The ability to make one's own recordings gives the student or instructor complete control of the prerecorded material as well as the ability to create new material. The British Open University has shifted much of its audio education to this format, citing (Bates, 1979), who notes that audio recordings are a more appropriate educational medium than radio:

- When the potential size of the class is too limited to recover the radio broadcast costs
- When analyzing or processing detailed visual material so that the cassette can "talk" the student through the material
- When repetition to obtain mastery in learning certain skills or techniques (such as the analysis of language, music structure and technique, or mathematical computations) is the purpose
- When analyzing or critically reviewing complex arguments or carefully structured logical arguments.

Additionally, its permanent nature allows the audio content to serve as reference and resource material and expands the possibilities of alternative and extended use of the information.

Because of its time-free, interruptable playback feature, the student has infinitely more control over the use of audio recordings than radio broadcast. One unique aspect of student control that audio recordings may provide is the flexibility of pacing through a course. A radio course or audio teleconference course usually requires that everyone progress through the material together, whereas the pacing of a course using time-free audio recordings can instead be designed around the learner's schedule.

One potential drawback of this medium, in addition to the more stringent copyright regulations mentioned above, is that the prerecorded material allows no opportunity for active interaction between student and instructor. To address this problem, the British Open University has experimented with having their tutors record their comments on student assignments for each student and then encourage the students to respond in the same way to their instructor's written and oral feedback. Although not fully interactive in the sense that no immediate conversation occurs, Kelly and Ryan (1983) report that students like these tutor tapes because they provide a degree of personal contact and allow for more critique, commentary, and review than would ordinarily appear in the tutor's written comments.

In the past decade, there has been a dramatic increase in the utilization of popular audiotape recordings, especially music, dramatic readings of literary classics and best-sellers, and how-to instructional and recreational programs. But unlike Great Britain, the acceptance in the United States of audiocassette courses for formalized education is still quite minimal. Its limited acceptance is due mainly to three factors: First, many instructors still feel that the use of audiovisual materials dilutes the rigor of a course. Second, if mediated instruction is offered by an institution, the more visually appealing video courses are often preferred over audio courses. Third, the lack of a sizable inventory of audio courses in the U.S. marketplace (fewer than fifty courses are available to a national market) has discouraged serious consideration of the medium. WHA-Radio and the University of Wisconsin are engaged in the production of a series (currently thirteen) of undergraduate-level, audio-print courses funded by the Annenberg/Corporation for Public Broadcasting Project. The development of a full curriculum of such academically rigorous courses is intended to increase the critical mass of inexpensive, credit-bearing courses designed for the nontraditional distant learner.

Audio Teleconferencing. This medium tries to address both issues of control and interaction by using combinations of broadcast lectures, audio recorded materials, and telephone conversations. Essentially, an audio teleconference is a telephone conversation among three or more individuals who can meet and interact on a real-time basis, not in a classroom, but electronically. By means of a speaker phone system and an electronic interconnection device called an audio bridge, participants at up to thirty distant sites can become a classroom group without requiring a classroom. Visual material to support the discussion can be mailed in advance to all sites or can be transmitted in a variety of ways over a second telephone line. A slow-scan video system transmits still video images (photos, charts, slides, images of three-dimensional objects like the speaker) over a narrowband phone channel to reception sites where the picture is reconstituted on a television monitor. A teletex facsimile transmits images of documents to sites equipped with decoder screens. An electronic blackboard enables handwriting or drawings done on an "electronic scratchpad" to be seen on television monitors at other sites. The immediate interactivity of this format creates a teaching-learning context that embodies all of the potential requirements of an effective educational medium—accessibility, quality, integration, control, and interactivity. Several states, such as Montana, Washington, Nevada, Iowa, Nebraska, and Wisconsin, have established operations from which international audio and statewide audio and visual teleconferences can take place. Rio Salado Community College in Phoenix, Arizona, uses audio teleconferencing with its radio courses to provide the distant learner with personal checkpoints during the semester and with orientation and course review sessions.

The Future

Even in the simple field of audio, technology is expanding and continuously being refined, which compounds the prospects for educational use. Tucker (1983) believes that the extension of educational opportunities created by these developments is also fostering a transformation of all aspects of education in the what, where, why, and how people teach and learn. Significantly, studies both in England and in the United States (Bates, 1981; Blackburn and Ging, 1986; Lewis, 1985) have found that it does not matter greatly to the student or the teacher which medium is used, as long as the quality and nature of the subject treatment through that medium is appropriate. This finding has important implications for the future of inexpensive, high-quality audio courses, which have for too long been considered subsidiary to video courses. The Center for the Study of Testing, Evaluation, and Educational Policy (CSTEEP, 1986) found that audio material enhanced the learning experience and the quality of university-level correspondence education because it reduced the distance and isolation of the independent learner. The challenge for audio-course faculty will be to recognize how changes in the teaching contexts (the nature and complexity of the subject matter) and the learning contexts (the abilities and needs of the students) can best be served by this medium.

The social and organizational dynamics of the new communications technology are creating new alliances of decision makers, new organizational communication patterns, new ways to evaluate performance and knowledge, new institutional consortia, and new budgetary requirements. Even audio is experiencing a renaissance in educational interests. As the medium becomes more popular and widely accepted, the issues surrounding its control, design, use, and implementation will increase. Ironically, in light of all of these complex changes, audio's strength has always rested in its simplicity, low cost, and accessibility. The test for the future will be to use the new electronic bridges made possible by modern technology to respond to the learner's needs, thus expanding the physical boundaries of the classroom, the psychological boundaries of student-teacher interaction, and the curricular boundaries of traditional education.

References

Bates, A. W. "Appropriate Teaching Functions for Television, Radio, and Audiocassettes in Open University Courses." Broadcast Subcommittee Publication. Milton Keynes: Open University, 1979.

Bates, A. W. "Radio: The Forgotten Medium: Executive Summary." Audiovisual Media Research Group Paper. Milton Keynes: Open University, 1981.

Bates, A. W., and Kern, L. "Alternative Media Technologies for the Open University: Final Report." Audiovisual Media Research Group Paper. Milton Keynes: Open University, 1977.

Blackburn, R. T., and Ging, T. *Faculty and Administrator's Use of Annenberg/CPB Project Video Courses*. Washington, D.C.: The Annenberg/CPB Project, 1986.

The Center for the Study of Testing, Evaluation, and Educational Policy (CSTEEP). *Final Report: Evaluation of the Audio Augmentation of College-Level Correspondence Courses*. Chestnut Hill, Mass.: Boston College, 1986.

Durbridge, N. "Audio Cassette." In A. W. Bates (ed.), *The Role of Technology in Distance Education*. London: Croom Helm, 1984.
Houle, C. O. *The Design of Education*. San Francisco: Jossey-Bass, 1972.
Kelly, P., and Ryan, S. "Using Tutor Tapes to Support the Distance Learner." *International Council for Distance Education Bulletin*, 1983, *3*, 1-18.
Lewis, R. J. *Faculty Perspectives on the Role of Informational Technology in Academic Institutions*. Washington, D.C.: The Annenberg/CPB Project, 1985.
Little, D. "Adult Learning and Education: A Concept Analysis." In P. Cunningham (ed.), *Yearbook of Adult and Continuing Education*. Chicago: Marquis Academic Media, 1979.
Reischmann, J. "Learning 'en passant': The Forgotten Dimension." Paper presented at the American Association of Adult and Continuing Education conference, Hollywood, Florida, October 23, 1986.
Riccobono, J. *Instructional Technology in Higher Education: A National Study of the Educational Uses of Telecommunications Technology in American Colleges and Universities*. Washington, D.C.: The Annenberg/CPB Project, 1986.
Ross, S. "Are We Creating an Information Elite?" *Technology and Society*, Winter 1982-83, p. 3.
Tucker, M. S. "The Turning Point: Telecommunications and Higher Education." In M. Kressel and P. J. Tate (eds.), *The Expanding Role of Telecommunications in Higher Education*. New Directions for Higher Education, no. 44. San Francisco: Jossey-Bass, 1983.
Wedemeyer, C. A. *Learning at the Back Door: Reflections on Nontraditional Learning in the Lifespan*. Madison: University of Wisconsin Press, 1981.

Patricia A. Takemoto is project administrator, the Annenberg/ Corporation for Public Broadcasting, Audio Core Curriculum Project, WHA-Radio, University of Wisconsin-Extension, Madison, Wisconsin.

As products and outcomes improve, interactive video, once rarely used, is gaining greater acceptance in education and training.

Interactive Video: The Present and the Promise

Kerry A. Johnson

As you push open the heavy glass door and enter the expansive, cool marble hall, you are overcome by several wonderful feelings. Never have you been alone with the paintings and sculpture before. Never have you been able to call on the insights of the masters or the critics to help you explore the richness of meaning behind the lustrous surfaces of the art, the motivations and the desires of the artists, or the intellectual energy of the works themselves. And never have you been able to call forth related works not presently on display in this museum. You are in control, free to wander in tune with your mood and thoughts, to question yourself and others about the most personal of ideas, or the most universal.

Less a physical activity than an intellectual exploration, this imaginary tour represents the potential of interactive video to bring an experience to life and place the control for that experience in the hands of the viewer. Interactive video is a medium derived from the marriage of the computer and the video. It is incredibly flexible, allowing for the harmonic blending of text, audio, and visual data bases in almost limitless combinations. It has been highly regarded since its introduction in the mid seventies because of its enormous potential in education and training. Yet it has not enjoyed the realization of that potential as quickly as was predicted.

Videodisc technology is similar to that of compact audiodiscs. The disc is read by laser, so there is virtually no physical wear. The 54,000 stored frames or visuals can be randomly accessed almost immediately or, when allowed to play uninterrupted, can provide thirty minutes of video and sixty minutes of audio. And, in its most powerful configuration, the videodisc can be combined with a computer to provide video, audio, computer graphics, and text on a single screen.

Interactive video is a complex medium, difficult to produce and, until recently, beyond the financial reach of most universities and corporate training divisions. However, besides production difficulty and cost, the chief factor that has limited wider use of interactive video has been the inability of educators and trainers to understand the range of possibilities for its use and, consequently, to create demand or funding sources for its development. Even the example of the art museum visit, while rich in possibilities, is only a partial glimpse of the true range of the medium. Limiting as it is, however, let us return to the art museum simulation to explore further the inherent power of interactive video.

On this particular day, you are feeling somewhat quiet. It is autumn, never your best season. If you examined your feelings by exploring the way others, particularly artists, expressed the same feelings, it might provide a useful insight into your own thoughts and suggest ways in which you could express your feelings better to yourself and others. Whatever the reason, it always seems to pleasant to be in the presence of favorite art or favorite artists on a quiet day.

In our scenario, you are standing in the marble hall and are approached by a docent who asks you what you would like to see. You are given several choices, all of which lead to other choices as the day progresses, and you decide to explore the theme of autumn and the changing of seasons. The gallery begins to open before you. You are particularly impressed by some American artists of the Hudson River School and their handling of the colors of the eastern mountains in fall, and so you decide to linger with them.

As you request visual details of various paintings, your mood gently shifts with the handling of the theme and you become fixed on a particular painting by Frederic Church called "The Great Fall, Niagara." You want to know more about it and its painter. You would certainly like to know basic things about the artist. For example, when did he paint "Niagara," and what was his age when he completed it? Perhaps you would also like to know something about the kind of person he was. And, of course, you would also like to know about this particular painting. Did he paint other paintings of the same scene? Did he make studies for this painting? If so, what do they look like? Where are they hung? How representative is this painting of his technique?

To get to all of this additional information about Church and his art, you engage in a dialogue with the system, perhaps through conversation with the docent or by selecting from a series of hierarchical menus that lead you deeper and deeper into the essence of a particular subject. You are in control of this experience, easily creating your own learning environment. You decide what and how you want to learn. You decide how long you can spend learning. The system adapts to your demands, guiding your experiences but never limiting them, even if that means leading you to external references.

Direct experience is admittedly invaluable, but there are many learning situations for which simulations are more appropriate than real experiences. For example, in a training environment where there might be a threat to individual safety or health or in a situation in which mistakes might be costly or irreversible, simulated experiences are preferable to actual experiences. Simulations are also a worthy substitute for reality where time or distance constrains first-hand experience, as is the case with the art tour. In these contexts, interactive video has demonstrated a virtually unparalleled ability to teach and challenge the learner via simulated experiences.

The Technology

This potential for stimulating self-directed learning is the result of a technology that has yet to be fully tapped. To understand this potential, educators need to look at three technical characteristics: (1) levels of interactivity, (2) technological evolution, and (3) instructional design requirements.

Levels of Interactivity. Nugent and his colleagues at the University of Nebraska are credited with devising what has become a very useful tool to describe the various types of interactive video. Three levels of interactive video are identified (Daynes and Butler, 1984). Level One interactive video consists of a stand-alone interactive video player. Control over the medium is accomplished with a keypad that provides random access to any of the 54,000 still-frame images on each side of the disc or to any running sequence of audiovisual material up to the thirty minutes available per side. It also provides separate access to each of the two sound tracks on the disc, if desired. Level One discs can be programmed with the keypad to allow the user a fixed sequence of material. Level One discs have many uses, but they are particularly valuable as traditional teaching aids, much like a videotape player or a slide projector.

Level Two interactive video contains preprogrammed materials. The program is incorporated onto the disc itself and is loaded into the memory of the videodisc player when the disc is played. This allows more complex programs to be developed than is possible using only a keypad. While Level Two discs have great promise, there are presently severe problems created by the lack of standardized formats that limit the use of the disc on multiple systems. Given the cost of pressing, or manufacturing, the disc itself, it is not reasonable under most conditions to consider making multiple versions of the same program. If these problems are overcome, the potential use of Level Two videodiscs will be greatly expanded. Certainly, Level Two provides an excellent teaching aid to enhance a seminar or lecture, and it also provides much more flexibility for independent learning of materials than Level One discs.

Level Three interactive video is exemplified in the art museum scenario. Level Three integrates the videodisc player with a computer, in essence putting the videodisc player under computer control. The majority of Level Three systems have used microcomputers. However, as the programs become more and more complex, greater demands are placed on the computer to manage, track, access, and deliver information, thereby clearly suggesting the benefits of larger, more powerful computers. Several computer corporations, notably Digital Equipment Corporation through its VAX family of computers, offer the option of interactive video in a mainframe environment.

Variations on the Level Three interactive video systems also involve combinations of peripherals such as touch screens, voice recognition, synthesized audio, and auxiliary storage devices such as CD ROM and compact discs. In addition to demonstrating where the technology is going, such variations suggest its roots. Clearly, interactive video is directly related to computer-based instruction (CBI). Production and design techniques reflect CBI experiences, and even a casual comparison with Carrier's chapter in this volume should confirm that conclusion. While there is significant influence from the video industry on the design and production of interactive video, the nonlinear capabilities of the medium are best realized by careful application of CBI development techniques.

Evolving Technologies. All early interactive video systems typically relied on customized hardware and software packages. The drawbacks of customized systems are obvious to anyone who has tried to produce and market instructional materials to a large organization or to several organizations. First, it is unlikely that any given university or corporate client will have the basic elements of the customized system: the specific hardware and software components that are at the heart of that customization. In addition, it is a characteristic of organizations that they will continue to work with a particular hardware or software vendor if they are satisfied with the service and performance and if the overall goals of the organization are being met by that vendor's products and services. What this means in practice is that, given a choice, individuals who select hardware and software systems for their university or company will be reluctant to support a new system, particularly a customized system that will be used only for specific training.

The technologies involved have been changing rapidly during the past few years. While the issue of standards has not been solved, there are many reasons to think that solutions are on the way. These hopeful signs come from related compact disc and CD ROM industries. Each of these industries is motivated by the need to access broad consumer markets that will make the investment in standardization worthwhile. Entry of the large computer companies into the interactive video market will certainly change the rules. Digital Equipment Corporation and National Cash Register Company gave considerable credibility to the medium, and now, with the entry of IBM, the way is clear for widespread imposition of standards. Even if the standards are market driven, they will clearly benefit the educational potential of this medium.

Design Requirements. Once the technological issues are understood, it is helpful to review two of the most critical issues involved in the design of interactive video. A more complete discussion of design issues, particularly video design issues, can be found in *The Videodisc Book: A Guide and Directory* (Daynes and Butler, 1984). In addition, although they refer primarily to computer-based instruction, Walker and Hess (1984) provide insights into topics such as improving student motivation, increasing interactivity, and designing simulations. Finally, perhaps the clearest and most succinct treatment of the design process appears in an article called "Courseware Development" by Lent (1986).

The single most important issue in ensuring a successful interactive video production is communication. Interactive video design and production must be a team activity. It requires the coordinated effort of specialists in at least four distinct areas: (1) instructional designers, (2) subject matter or content specialists, (3) video producers, and (4) computer programmers. What makes team communication difficult is that team members' differing backgrounds lead them to conceptualize and to solve problems in different ways. As team members work together to design and produce the final product, their conversations must be continually translated and interpreted by the team leader so that everyone proceeds toward the same goals.

A return to the art museum scenario for a moment will clarify this point. As a visitor to the gallery, you have an apparently limitless set of choices. Like the physical reality of the gallery itself, this is an illusion, since in truth all computer-based simulations have limits. However, it is possible through clever instructional design to minimize those limitations, but it is only possible to create a clever design if communications among team members can bridge the respective gaps of knowledge and experience.

For example, by exploring the use of special video techniques and communicating those techniques to the design team, the video producer can offer new opportunities for describing painting styles or the technical aspects of composition that neither the content specialist, the programmer, nor the designer might have seen. Similarly, by understanding the capabilities of an authoring environment and relating that to the geography of the videodisc, a programmer might save the designers and video producers time and help the team avoid costly duplication of effort late in a project's life cycle. But the programmer can only accomplish this if he or she understands the basics of video editing and can communicate this technical knowledge in nontechnical terms.

The key role in establishing effective, efficient communication links within the project team is generally played by the instructional designer. Because of his or her broad, comprehensive understanding of design and technical requirements, the instructional designer is in a unique position to interpret and translate the special language and knowledge of all members of the project team so that each can benefit from the insights of the others. The instructional designer, therefore, becomes the natural leader of the project team.

A second major design requirement is the team's ability to envision potential interactions between the ultimate user and the learning system as multidimensional events. People think much more quickly and flexibly than computers—if computers can be considered to think at all. As a result, it is extremely difficult to predict the direction a student is likely to take when using the instructional materials. In designing those materials, it is therefore crucial to anticipate as many learning paths as possible. The design team must map those possibilities in advance and then keep a balance between those conceptual maps and the capabilities of the system to adequately reproduce the maps. The failure to create complex instructional maps results in programs that rely on limited choices—programs driven by responses to closed questions, like multiple-choice or true-false questions.

In contrast to the earlier art museum simulation, it is clear that an experience driven by multiple-choice questions, no matter how marvelous the visual, will become tedious and mundane. Certainly there are many contexts in which this drill-and-practice approach is sufficient. But, to use the technology to its fullest advantage—to be alive—the environment created through the interactive video must be multidimensional. It must challenge the user. It must allow the user to challenge it. It must invite and excite in a personal way. Most important, it must surprise. It order to create such an environment, the design team must be able to anticipate the learner, just as any good writer anticipates the reactions of the reader.

Applications and Alternatives

Writing about interactive video in higher education, Nugent (1982) was able to present a comprehensive picture of the state of the art by describing what a handful of universities were doing. Today, barely five years later, the number and variety of projects, both in education and training, defy easy description (for example, see Bayard-White, 1985; Bosco, 1986; Bove, 1986). Certainly the fictional example of the visit to an art museum provides an illustration of interactive video's potential, but there is a wide range of real examples that also characterize the present state of the art. With the author's apologies to the many excellent programs that will not be mentioned, a few examples of creative uses being made of this flexible medium are presented below.

Independent Learning. The National Agriculture Library (NAL) is responsible for providing information services to the nation's agriculture industry. In addition, they are required to provide up-to-date data, references, and information services to the world's agriculture data bases. NAL has always maintained traditional library facilities but has moved aggressively during the past decade to computerize its reference system. One result of this effort has been the creation of the agriculture data base called AGRICOLA. AGRICOLA references most American agriculture publications and a great many foreign publications as well.

With the rising sophistication of its information services, NAL also noticed increased problems with user education. Many individuals who access AGRICOLA are either not computer literate or are unfamiliar with the specific requirements of this particular data base. What they need is information about some agriculture problem, and they generally need it quickly. NAL did not want them to be confounded by a system intended for frequent use.

Thus, NAL felt that a training system in the use of AGRICOLA, as well as in general strategies for searching on-line data bases, was necessary. The instructional problem was summarized as follows:

- Many learners were located at multiple sites
- Learners needed frequent use of AGRICOLA
- Some learners had little computer experience
- Traditional training took too much learner time
- Traditional training required too much staff time
- Resources for training were scarce
- NAL had a strong desire to increase use of AGRICOLA.

To meet this training need, NAL formed a cooperative partnership with the University of Maryland through the Center for Instructional Development and Evaluation (CIDE) at University College and the College of Library and Information Services at the College Park campus. The goal of this partnership was to create a short, comprehensive instructional package that could be used in an independent study format by a variety of audiences. NAL's strong commitment to expand access to AGRICOLA provided essential motivation for creating the cooperative agreement.

The interactive video package was designed to culminate in a simulation of a series of typical on-line search experiences guided by a mentor who accompanies the user on the search. The user is encouraged to ask questions of the mentor as difficulties are encountered in accessing the data base or completing a search. In addition, the exercises are structured so that experienced reference users can skip quickly to relevant material.

Video and audio are used throughout this instructional package to motivate the learner, as would occur in a one-on-one environment, as well as to enhance certain points and clarify particular concepts. Computer-generated graphics are combined with text in situations where a powerful, realistic visual would make the point more quickly than written discourse alone.

Tradition Meets Technology. A different, but equally powerful use of interactive video is being made by Alcoa at its Tennessee plant. While this activity is not taking place outside the classroom, it is certainly innovative and bears mention. Instructors at the Tennessee facilities are using training materials created for them by Digital Equipment Corporation's Adaptive Learning Solutions (ALS) group. Working in conjunction with Alcoa subject-matter specialists, ALS created a dynamic and powerful teaching environment that is highly interactive, completely portable, and very flexible.

The class, arranged in a U-shaped conference room, faces an instructor standing in front of a large video projection screen. The interactive video system is accessed in several ways. One terminal is set with its screen in a horizontal position, in essence creating for the instructor an electronic teaching station. Teaching notes and audiovisual aids are all included in the single integrated system. As the instructor moves through the complex technical material in a well-choreographed, professional manner, the materials the instructor selects are projected onto the screen. All instructors come from the plant floor. They are technicians, not teachers, and yet the presentations are flawless. Confidently drawing from the scripted materials, they regularly add their own anecdotes, cautions, and advice. As questions arise, the instructor uses the random access capabilities of the medium to call forth relevant segments of video or a set of slides or computer graphics, integrating them seamlessly.

At a point when it is important to practice some of the skills or apply some of the concepts, the class is divided into small groups of three or four around the interactive video learning stations set up in the room. The groups engage in animated discussion of various points. They encounter simulated situations involving potentially dangerous and real problems they will be expected to handle on the job. They are assessed, and they discover what they need to know or do in order to improve their performance. Later on, their instructor is able to provide additional feedback by examining student performance data and patterns.

Repurposing Old Media. The Health Services Command of the U.S. Navy, long respected for its use of instructional media, decided a few years ago that interactive video was an appropriate, effective medium for training medical corpsmen. They also had at their disposal a tremendous number of high-quality training films. It seemed reasonable to expect that these existing materials could be reused in the interactive video format, even if only at Level One. After transferring eight of their films to disc, however, they began to consider their potential for nonclassroom purposes and solicited the help of the University of Maryland's Center for Instructional Development and Evaluation (CIDE).

CIDE has taken these linear films, all in the basic areas of anatomy and physiology, and turned them into a highly interactive set of review materials for Navy corpsmen. Their instructional goal is to provide a link between the material covered in a traditional lecture/laboratory and the situations faced by the corpsmen on duty. By using the video material available from the films and integrating it with a package designed to allow for branching and interactivity, the corpsmen may query the materials to search for answers to questions that arise either in the classroom or on the job.

What was formerly linear, group-oriented instructional material has now become that and much more. In the independent learning situation, it provides ready reference, review, and refresher; in the classroom, it offers random access video for teacher use. And, of great significance to development costs, the most expensive aspect of interactive video, the video production, has been virtually eliminated by repurposing existing video.

Expanding the Interactivity. The 1986 Nebraska Videodisc Award for Best Overall Achievement, presented to Ixion and the Academy of Aeronautics for "The Academy of Aeronautics Welding Simulator," moves the state of interactive video art to a still higher level. After an extensive tutorial—based entirely on clear, icon and picture-based menus; practice; and help—the student engages in a realistic simulation. Using an input device that simulates a welding torch, the student encounters typical welding situations, and responds to them through the interactive video system. The video monitor is placed in a horizontal plane for this exercise. Through the attachment of a three-dimensional touch screen, the space above the monitor becomes a welding environment sensitive to the position and movement of the torch. As the student moves the simulated torch, the weld appears instantly as a video image changing in relation to the position and speed of the torch.

The student's complete control of this simulated environment is consistent with reality—the user owns the success and the consequences of his or her action. Feedback is instant, realistic, nonthreatening, and helpful. Learning cost, at least in terms of materials, is minimal. And transfer between the learning task and the job is direct. The materials represent the closest approximation yet to the experience of being an apprentice working directly with a master, learning as one works, working as one learns.

Developing Designers

The complex nature of interactive video production together with a review of a few examples of current projects in the field, has been discussed in this chapter. Nevertheless, an important question remains: Where does one find the people to do it? Certainly many of the traditional instructional design programs have begun to provide the necessary training, but the numbers of designers who will be needed in the next ten years will likely outpace the output of the existing programs. One new, unique program is particularly worth noting, however, and that is the program at Bloomsburg University.

Bloomsburg has a master's degree program completely devoted to training students to apply instructional system design theory to the development of interactive video. The current enrollment of sixty demonstrates the existing interest in the field. The curriculum has been designed with sufficient rigor to turn out competent professionals. To prepare for future professional roles, students in the Bloomsburg program have a unique opportunity in that each is required to complete an entire interactive video project for graduation.

These graduation projects are funded either by the university through its Instructional Systems Center and faculty grants or by external, client-supported projects in the center. Production budgets are kept small by using low-cost production techniques. The center owns Panasonic eight-inch videodisc production equipment on which it can produce a disc for about $180. This compares with a price of $2,000 for professionally pressing a regular twelve-inch videodisc.

Materials produced through student projects in the Bloomsburg program are presently being used in courses in special education, chemistry, and art. Many more projects are planned or are underway. Given the promise of this already flourishing young program and the predicted need in the field, who can doubt that enrollments will continue to climb and similar programs at other universities will soon be established? After all, society is witnessing the beginnings of a highly creative profession that will be likely to draw from the same pool of individuals who are currently attracted by careers in film, video, art, and theater. The one advantage that the instructional design professions will offer over those fields is the likelihood of more stable salaries and job possibilities.

Potentials and Limitations

There seems little doubt, given the rapidly rising use of interactive video, that it will eventually play a major role in education and training. The projects described above give some indication of the current uses and the current promise; the art museum provides a sense of the future and the potential. But what is the relationship between the potential and the limitations?

As it has been woven throughout the narrative, the example of the art museum has been admittedly comprehensive and, while it may seem far-fetched, in fact the technology for each piece is already in place and can be used today. What keeps individuals from doing so now are money, markets, and materials.

The costs of producing interactive video remain high, but that is not really the significant issue. For instance, business and government will spend about $4.5 billion on video production this year, and the larger percentage of this money is spent by training departments (Bove, 1986). Also, the expense of producing the disc itself is negligible in relation to the cost of the video production; courseware design, development, and programming contribute most to total project costs. This leaves the incorrect impression that interactive video is significantly more expensive to produce than other well-designed instructional systems.

While interactive video is admittedly expensive to produce, in fact, there is a danger of using the wrong frame of reference to compare costs and benefits. A new view is required, one that does not simply add the costs of one medium and hold them directly against those of another—in this case, typically comparing interactive video with traditional face-to-face instruction. First, the costing models are different. Interactive video costs primarily occur prior to instruction, while costs for traditional media courses are more evenly distributed over the life of the course. Second, thoughtful design should lead to a different set of benefits for each approach. Interactive video and traditional instruction are different means to different ends and therefore should not be considered mutually exclusive, either-or choices. And, finally, if the cost analysis has something to do with meaningful learner contact time, long-term use of the instruction must be calculated. In this type of analysis, interactive video fairs well.

Development of markets for interactive video is related to several interdependent factors, among which are sales volume and standardization. In order to bring equipment costs down, the hardware industry must have high-volume sales. In order to buy in volume, consumers must be assured of standardization across manufacturers. There are many examples of this phenomenon, from microcomputers to compact discs, and while the same companies seem eager to standardize their other technologies, they have been slow to do so with videodisc.

A related issue involves the availability of materials to use with interactive video systems. Certainly there is some very high-quality courseware being produced. The examples presented here give ample evidence of that. However, the quantity of quality, general purpose materials is presently insufficient to encourage the market to move rapidly. In addition, there is a shortage of skilled producers who truly understand the potential of the medium and the needs of the market.

However, these current limits on interactive video are temporary. They affect pace, not promise. In fact, there are no real limits at all to what can be accomplished, once the costs are understood, the markets are established, and a minimal, yet critical mass of materials is available.

Meanwhile, creative designers and producers are pushing the technology forward for ever more sophisticated users. Much is expected from interactive video and its proponents will not be disappointed.

References

Bayard-White, C. *Interactive Video Case Studies and Directory.* London: Council for Educational Technology, 1985.

Bosco, J. "An Analysis of Evaluations of Interactive Video." *Educational Technology,* 1986, *26* (5), 7-17.

Bove, R. "Video Training: The State of the Industry." *Training and Development Journal,* 1986, *40* (8), 27-29.

Daynes, R., and Butler, B. *The Videodisc Book: A Guide and Directory.* New York: Wiley, 1984.

Lent, R. "Courseware Development." *National Forum,* 1986, *66* (3), 15-18.

Nugent, R. W. "Videodiscs and Learning." In C. K. Knapper (ed.), *Expanding Learning Through New Communications Technologies.* New Directions for Teaching and Learning, no. 9. San Francisco: Jossey-Bass, 1982.

Walker, D. F., and Hess, R. D. (eds.). *Instructional Software: Principles and Perspectives for Design and Use.* Belmont, Calif.: Wadsworth, 1984.

Kerry A. Johnson is director, Center for Instructional Development and Evaluation, University of Maryland.

Print has long been the most popular medium for learning outside the classroom. The most important techniques of teaching through print are the correspondence study guide and self-directed learning text. Much is being learned from both American and international experience and research about the design of printed courses and their use as a basis for teaching adults.

Print Media

Michael G. Moore

Print Media as Distance Education

As a medium of instruction, printed communication predates the other media described in this volume. While instruction by print alone has proven successful in almost every nation for more than a century, seldom has any other medium been entirely satisfactory unaided; other media are more effective when supplemented, or perhaps organized around, a printed text or study guide. In large distance education systems, such as the British Open University, instruction is provided not only through print but also through broadcast media, audio-and videotapes, teletext and view data systems, personal computer, and telephone, to name only the most common. The overwhelming majority of students elect to devote the greatest part of their study time to the printed text and the study guide, with its associated written assignments. The print medium is undoubtedly the most popular medium. It is familiar and, generally, inexpensive. It is the ideal medium around which, and through which, to organize other media. Only the print media that meet the following criteria will be included in this chapter:

1. Those designed with the primary purpose of changing a person's knowledge, skills, or values in a positive direction.
2. Those designed in such a way that the learner consents to the direction of change.

3. Those designed to communicate not only information and ideas (content) but also guidance on learning, advice on study, devices to sustain the learner's motivation, and assistance in their self-assessment—that is, the communication focuses on the *process* of learning as well as the content.

Educational print media that meet the above criteria are of two main types: correspondence study guides and didactic texts prepared for the self-directed learners. Of these, by far the most important because of the numbers of learners, educators, and institutions that use them is the correspondence study guide. Although these two types of teaching-by-print have many features in common, there is a fundamental difference between them: Study guides direct a series of interactions between the learner and a human instructor, whereas didactic texts are designed to be self-sufficient and independent of external instruction.

Distance education is a term that has come into prominence in recent years—but was used as long ago as 1892 in the University of Chicago Calendar—to describe all educational situations in which the activities of instructing and those of learning take place apart, so that communication is by print, electronics, or other means. The distance between learner and instructor is not merely geographic but refers also to educational distance, the extent to which the learner is able to interact on an individual basis with the instructor.

Recent History of Teaching by Print

In 1938, representatives of five nations met in Victoria, Canada, to found the International Council on Correspondence Education. By 1965, Johnstone and Rivera (1965) found nearly 2 million adults participating in correspondence courses in the United States. Sivatko (1969) estimated that the total number of U.S. citizens who had studied by correspondence by the year 1969 was over 75 million. The most recent information on correspondence in the university sector shows some seventy-one U.S. universities providing instruction to about 250,000 newly enrolled students during the year 1981-82. The largest of these is Brigham Young University, with 17,500 annual enrollments, followed by these universities: Missouri, Nebraska, Indiana, Pennsylvania State, Texas Technical, Wisconsin, Louisiana State, Minnesota, and California. According to Holbrook (1982), to those who study by correspondence with universities and colleges should be added some 600,000 students in private correspondence schools and 600,000 in the military.

In the 1960s, when Prime Minister Harold Wilson of Great Britain ordered his education officials to open up and democratize higher education in that country, they discovered at the University of Wisconsin a project called the Articulated Instructional Media (AIM) project. This was a

Carnegie-funded experiment to link up (articulate) various teaching methods and media to the central medium of correspondence education to teach off-campus students. As well as correspondence study guides, methods included short periods of residential study, use of local library resources, and use of radio, TV, and telephone conferences. Courses were developed by teams of academics, media personnel, and course designers. In 1969, C. A. Wedemeyer, director of AIM, was invited to England to share in designing a new higher education system based on the AIM project. The British decision was to establish a fully autonomous Open University. Although employing a range of media, it had, and continues to have, correspondence instruction as the basis of its teaching system. About 3 million course packages are sent out from the Open University each year, and nearly 1 million student assignments are submitted and marked. Since its inception, 250,000 people have studied with the university, and each year some 100,000 students take courses. The success of this institution has revived the practice of correspondence education, spread the method around the world, and initiated a renaissance of study, research, and scholarship in this previously neglected field.

Within a decade of the founding of the Open University, similar institutions were established in Spain, Israel, West Germany, Canada, Pakistan, Venezuela, Costa Rica, and Thailand. More recently, open universities have been started in the Netherlands, Sri Lanka, Hong Kong, and Japan. Representative of other important institutions that are not fully autonomous universities but that use correspondence education in many ways similar to the open universities, are Deakin University in Australia, British Columbia's Open Learning Institute, and the Correspondence and Open Studies Institute at the University of Lagos in Nigeria. In the United States at the present time, two significant developments are evident. The first is the stimulus given to the development of distance education methods and programs as a result of the work of the Annenberg/CPB Project. Perhaps the most important work done by the project has been to initiate and stimulate a program of research both evaluative and basic. The second major development of recent years has been the creation of networks and consortia for delivering distance education. This is seen most dramatically in the International University Consortium for Telecommunications in Learning. This network of twenty-one colleges and universities, in partnership with local television or cable stations, aims to deliver a nationwide program on a scale beyond the resources of any of the partners acting alone. The network that is evolving has most, if not all, of the features of a formally established open education system; in particular, there is the use of several media based on a print study guide and a quasi-industrial system of course design and instruction that uses specialization and large scale investment.

Some Recent Research in Teaching Through Print Media

The scholar who has been the most consistent reviewer and reporter of research in distance education in recent years is B. Holmberg, a Swedish national who is professor of research in distance education at the Fernuniversitat in Hagen, Germany. He has developed a theory about the method of distance education that he calls guided didactic conversation. This theory suggests that the character of good print teaching materials is that of a guided conversation aimed at learning and that the presence of the typical traits of such a conversation facilitates learning. In his most recent survey of research in distance education, which covered research in the last decade, Holmberg cites about twenty different research studies concerning the design and structure of print materials. Only a few representative studies may be mentioned here, and the reader is referred to Holmberg (1982, pp. 19-31). There have been studies of the relative effectiveness of placing questions before a passage of text, inserted into it, or placed after it; studies have also been made of such grammatical variables as the active compared with the passive voice, affirmative compared with negative statements, and abstract compared with concrete nouns. Some studies have found that comprehension decreases as adjectives increase but that pronouns communicate the message more easily. Communications with more pronouns have been found to be easier to understand, which is attributed to that fact that they stimulate personal interest. Prepositions have been found to decrease comprehension; the more prepositions, the more difficult the communication.

At the British Open University, MacDonald-Ross (1979) has specialized in the study and research of readability formulae and has used word length and frequency, sentence length, and similar measures to predict reading difficulty. He indicates that there is a clear relationship between readability and learner acceptability as well as between readability and efficiency of reading. Kare and Smart (1973) found a rank-order correlation of 0.87 between the readability level of correspondence material and the probability that students would send in all their lessons (with length held constant).

Studies have been made of the optimum balance between density of information in a text and elaboration of that information. Taylor (1977, p. 25) states, "The effective communicator elaborates his discourse. He identifies the novel and more difficult concepts. He gives examples. He rephrases his exposition and provides repetition. When the amount of elaboration is low, the presentation is considered difficult. As elaboration increases, the discourse gets easier for the subject. Up to 30 percent elaboration reduces presentation difficulty. When the amount of elaboration exceeds 30 percent, the presentation gets more difficult." Techniques have been developed to direct students' attention to important issues and to considering and searching for solutions, and there is both research and considerable debate on the value of such techniques. Some fear that attention directors may divert students' interest from the content to the technical aspects of the reading process and thus encourage surface learning and lead to neglect of deep structure learning. There is a wealth of literature on graphic design, and the Institute of Education Technology (IET) of the Open University has published a comprehensive bibliography. The journal *Instructional Science* devoted a whole volume to graphic communication in 1979.

The above examples are intended to raise in the reader an awareness that not only is teaching through print different from other forms of writing but the body of knowledge of how to teach through print is based on an active field of research as well as many years of experience.

Course Design

The most common model for course development is the author-editor model. Authors (often professors) are contracted to write a course, which is then edited by specialists within the correspondence school or independent studies department.

According to Smith's (1980) explanation, at Pennsylvania State University course development is primarily the responsibility of the Department of Independent Study by Correspondence (DISC). Writer-editors supplemented by part-time specialists work with full-time faculty of the university in the planning and development of both credit and noncredit courses. The writing of courses by the staff of academic departments is once again done on an overload basis and is not an integral part of normal teaching responsibilities. In most cases, the correspondence material consists of units that include a statement of lesson objectives, a reading assignment, a commentary and a study guide, and a written assignment to be completed. Editors work with the textbook and study guide, and if the guides do not elucidate sufficiently, revisions are suggested to the authors concerned.

The role of the editors is more comprehensive than merely responding to the draft material. They provide a service to the authors that includes clearance of copyright, location of relevant photographs and other graphic material, and the ordering of tapes and other audiovisual elements; they also suggest appropriate formats to facilitate the learning process.

Courses currently being developed with Annenberg/CPB Project funding and those of the Consortium for Telecommunication in Learning consist not only of study guides, set books, and student assessments but also video and audio programs, either broadcast or on tape, as well as contact with faculty members through mail or telephone in the participating institutions. Despite these efforts, the quality of print materials in

American distance education programs has not improved at the same pace as the development of other media nor is it as good as the print materials produced in some other countries.

The differences between the products of the American university and the British Open University are largely a result of the differences in the scale of the operations. The Open University employs a faculty of some 700 people whose primary occupation is the design, development, and delivery of distance education programs. Between one and two million dollars are invested in each course. In what Professor Peters, rector of West Germany's Feruniversitat called "the industrial form of education," courses are never designed by only one person nor are they taught by the same people who designed them. There is a division of labor, with different academics taking responsibility for content in their special areas of expertise. Educational technologists guide the design and writing of study guides and correspondence texts, evaluation materials, and instructional devices, and continuing educators pay attention to the ways in which the material will be used by the learner. Courses are prepared by teams of ten to twenty specialists over a period of two years and then taught to several thousand students a year with a different team of instructors providing the correspondence instruction. The products that make up an Open University course are all print materials, with the exception of TV and radio programs, records and tapes, and experimental kits. Each course typically consists of thirty-two correspondence units, each being studied by the student over a one-week period and all thirty-two making up the full year's course. Each correspondence unit might be written by a different academic, and all course products might be prepared by different academics and education technologists.

Simpler course team models have evolved in other countries. At Athabasca University in Canada, for example, the course team consists of just one academic, one educational technologist, an editor, a visual designer, and a media consultant. This results in only one scholar's perception of the content being taught, and thus there is likely to be some loss of breadth and depth as a result. However, it is a far less expensive system than that of the Open University. At Athabasca University, courses are in the form of study guides containing working directions for the students, self-test questions, assignments, and information about final assessment. Each unit is divided into sections that, in turn, are divided into a number of specific objectives. From time to time, students are directed to other readings outside the course material, and when all readings for the objectives are completed, practice questions and exercises are provided, together with a self-test at the end of each unit. A list of references and further readings is given at the end of each unit. To show the relationship of one section of a unit to another and to the unit as a whole, concept maps are used at the beginning of each section. Evaluation of each unit and of the course as a whole is built in as an automatic process of the course development procedure.

The U.S., Canadian, and British courses that have been referred to all have the following elements in common:
1. Course materials are all related to specific objectives, which are presented to the student in the beginning of the course.
2. Final or summative evaluation measures the student's achievement of the objectives of the course.
3. Evaluation during the life of the course (formative evaluation) gives the student an idea of his or her progress and in some institutions contributes to the student's final grade.
4. Each unit includes a reading assignment usually found in a reader associated with the course although sometimes contained in the body of the course itself.
5. Each unit contains a commentary on the reading.
6. Each unit contains guidance to the student to help the student deal with the content of the readings.
7. Each course contains a number of required written assignments that the student submits, which provide the basis of instruction from the correspondence instructor.

Good correspondence study guides have certain characteristics in common. First, they are very carefully structured. A good course is designed to reflect the structure of the field of knowledge with which it deals. Concepts should be presented first in a comparatively simple way. The student may be brought back to them later when, helped by a sense of familiarity, he or she will be able to understand new and more difficult interpretations of the concept being dealt with. This means that the course will be easier to follow and more effective when it has a number of themes running through it. These themes and their structure should be clear to the student. It is especially important that students not be faced at the beginning of the course with material beyond their ability. This is when drop-out rates are at their highest. Similarly, care should be taken before allowing any sudden increase in difficulty, since this will discourage distance learners. Good structure also refers to the style of the various parts of the printed teaching materials: the expression of general aims and specific objectives, self-tests, assignment questions, and examinations. Structure requires a reasonable conformity among authors regarding such matters as terminology and teaching style. Personal idiosyncrasies are permissible and to be encouraged, but the general style has to be such that the student develops a sense of overall purpose and consistency. Good structure also demands that nonprint or supplementary material is well-integrated with print material. If there are broadcasts, audiotapes, or class sessions, each course unit needs reference to the use so that the students understand how the various elements fit together. It is very important that these supplementary materials are conceived and prepared as an integral part of the course, not added on after the written materials have been completed.

A second key concept of course design is self-sufficiency. The correspondence student works alone, and while some institutions provide face-to-face instruction as an ancillary to printed materials, participation in face-to-face instruction should not be assumed. Many students are not able to or do not want to participate, and courses therefore must be designed to be self-sufficient. Furthermore, it is desirable, and unusual, for each unit of a course to stand by itself. This gives the student a sense of accomplishment when working through the course.

The course should guide the student on written or practical work. Like a good teacher, the study guide should offer encouragement. Where a course uses a text as well as a study guide, the guide may have to fill in the gaps left where the textbook does not fit what the course writer wants to do (Perraton, 1973). Study notes consist of statements that explain, clarify, augment, or correct those made in the textbook. Study notes are often keyed to the page numbers of the textbook for easy reference.

Courses must be geared to the student's isolated situation. Many correspondence students do not have access to the range of books open to school students, and adult students are apt to interpret suggestions for further study as required reading. Open University courses aim to be entirely self-sufficient and to require no reading by the student outside the materials provided by the course. One last sequence of the need to be self-sufficient is to provide, within the course information, information on how to obtain assistance or otherwise deal with problems that cannot be solved in isolation. The student should be directed to write to the correspondence tutor or to telephone the distance education institution.

A third characteristic of the printed study guide is that it should have personality. Every effort should be made to convey to the student the sense of excitement, discovery, and satisfaction that motivates those who write the course. Many academics are not able to write in a way that is both intelligible and stimulating, and making materials exciting is an important challenge for the educational technologist and adult educators who, with the academics, produce the course (Lewis, 1971). An impersonal style is inappropriate. Courses are usually written in the first person, and the student is addressed directly as "you." Writing to the distance student, one needs, above all else, to be clear and very straightforward. The study guide is not the place to show off one's own knowledge. It is better to over-simplify in order to remain clear than to risk confusing the student. On the other hand, teaching in print will be more stimulating when there is variety in the writing. Thus, a unit might open in a conversational or colloquial style but move into more subtle, precise, and formal language as it discusses the complexities of the subject.

To these well-established ideas about teaching by print, a new key concept has recently emerged. This is the idea of learner contribution. The typical distance education course is so highly structured that it gives the student little autonomy. The student may choose from a range of courses but then must follow a precise sequence of materials, omitting very little and bringing in very little personal experience. The course writers determine the subject of the assignments to be written by the student and prepare a guide as to what the student should have written. While high academic standards might be maintained by such standardization and quality-control techniques, students can receive the impression that knowledge is passive and unproblematic, something bought in a package like a commodity. New efforts are being made to structure the printed course to allow enough space for students to explore outside the course, to use their own experience, and to bring their own self-discovered knowledge to the course. Courses are now available in which the written assignment has been replaced by a learner-designed project, negotiated through correspondence, in which students are able to apply and test principles explained in the course in their own home or work settings. This trend to incorporate project work, discovery learning, and even peer teaching at a distance—in short, to develop greater learner independence—is one of the most important developments in distance education at the present time.

The Instructor

Most distance education institutions rely on written correspondence between student and personal instructor. Those who design teaching texts include in them a number of questions or assignments the student is expected to work on and send to the instructor. The instructor's job is to offer criticism and advice with reference to the various texts. The instructor, therefore, has to be thoroughly knowledgeable about all aspects of the printed material but, as an academic, must also be prepared to be critical and to some extent independent of this material. Specific references to particular passages in the text are a valuable and economical way of expanding advice to the student; at the same time, the student should be helped to develop a critical view of the course material. It is particularly challenging for the distant instructor to engage with the student in dialogue, controversy, and even disagreement. The instructor's comments need to be very carefully phrased and considerate since the opportunity for added explanation is not available as in a face-to-face setting. It is essential that the instructor does everything to prevent demoralization, and he or she must make every effort to avoid an abrupt or curt style. The correspondence instructor has to learn to raise the issues that are indicated by the print study guide with the distant and largely unknown student and to do this in a way that conveys an air of cooperation and friendliness. It is apparent that the relationship among the course designer, writers, instructors, and learners is a very subtle one. It has already been the subject of considerable research, but is worthy of a great deal more.

Summary

This chapter has provided a very brief review of printed communication as a medium for instructing adults outside the classroom. Of the two main types of such instruction, correspondence texts and didactic texts designed for self-directed learners, only the former has been discussed here. Teaching through print has assumed new importance in recent years as it has been incorporated into multimedia distance education systems, the best known of which is the British Open University. In large distance education systems, printed courses are prepared by teams of specialists. The characteristics looked for in printed courses include good structure, self-sufficiency, personality, and attention to learner autonomy. Producing courses is only one part of the business of teaching through print; equally important is the interaction between instructor and learner that occurs through correspondence.

References

Holbrook, D. "Accreditation, a Workable Option." In J. S. Daniel, M. A. Stroud, and J. R. Thompson (eds.), *Learning at a Distance*. Edmonton, Alberta: Athabasca University, 1982.

Holmberg, B. *Recent Research into Distance Education*. Hagen, West Germany: Zentrales Institut fur Fernstudienforschung, 1982.

Johnstone, J., and Rivera, R. *Volunteers for Learning: A Study of the Educational Pursuits of American Adults*. Chicago: Aldine, 1965.

Kare, G. R., and Smart, K. "Analysis of the Readability Level of Selected USAFI Instructional Materials." *Journal of Educational Research*, 1973, 67, 176.

Lewis, B. N. "Course Production at the Open University II: Activities and Activity Networks." *British Journal of Education Technology*, 1971, 2 (2), 111.

MacDonald-Ross, M. "Language in Texts: A Review of Research Relevant to the Design of Curricular Materials." In L. S. Shulman (ed.), *Review of Research in Education*. Itasca, Ill.: Peacock, 1979.

Perraton, H. *The Techniques of Writing Correspondence Courses*. IEC Broadsheet on Distance Learning, no. 2. Cambridge, England: International Extension College, 1973.

Sivatko, J. "Correspondence Instruction." In E. R. Ebel (ed.), *Encyclopedia of Education Research*. 4th ed. New York: Macmillan, 1969.

Smith, K. C. "Course Development Procedures." *Distance Education*, 1980, *1* (1), 61-62.

Taylor, F. J. "Acquiring Knowledge from Prose and Continuous Discourse." In M.J.A. Howe (ed.), *Adult Learning: Psychological Research and Application*. London: Wiley, 1977.

Michael G. Moore is associate professor of adult education, Pennsylvania State University.

Technology will allow instruction to be delivered to adults in many locations at any time of the day or night.

Computers in Adult Learning Outside the Classroom

Carol A. Carrier

Sara Lad, a full-time dental hygienist, has located her computer in a small den just off her kitchen. While waiting for her dinner to cook, Sara calls up a computerized catalogue and browses through the electronics section. She is shopping for a new amplifier for her stereo system. On her screen, she views the various amplifiers and reads descriptions of their features. With her audio device she listens to samples of sound from the different amps. Before returning to the kitchen to eat, Sara remembers to call up her weekly electronic calender and adds to it a Tuesday night appointment.

After dinner Sara must work on her extension class assignment. She returns to her den and uses her computer to dial her extension class hookup. She receives feedback from the instructor on an earlier assignment and reviews the guidelines for the next one. This assignment requires that Sara first work through a computer-based tutorial on several money and banking principles and read a chapter from the course text. She will then ask for the questions she must

J. A. Niemi, D. D. Gooler (eds.). *Technologies for Learning Outside the Classroom.*
New Directions for Continuing Education, no. 34. San Francisco: Jossey-Bass, Summer 1987. 51

answer and send back to the instructor through the network. At 10:30 P.M. Sara turns off the system, feeling satisfied with her progress on the class assignment.

A futuristic scenario? Not at all. Microcomputers and related technology have made experiences like Sara's possible. In truth, microcomputers have invaded our lives in force. During the 1985/86 academic year, an estimated $680 million was spent on hardware and software for computer education (Reinhold, 1986). Beginning in 1982, Dartmouth College strongly recommended that all incoming freshmen purchase their own microcomputers. Zemke (1984) reports that half of the Fortune 500 companies surveyed used some form of computer-assisted training. Microcomputers have also found a place in the home.

This chapter focuses primarily on computer-based educational experiences for adults that occur outside the formal classroom. It begins with a discussion of principles of adult learning that are likely to affect the use of technology-based learning experiences. It then moves to an overview of how computer technology is used in a variety of contexts for adult learning. The concluding section highlights issues that affect the potential uses of computers and related technologies in nonformal settings.

Computers and the Adult Learner

High school and college graduations are celebrated events that for many people bring to an end a long period of structured learning experiences. At this point, the individual launches into the world of work. This transition also marks the beginning of different types of incentives for learning, such as career advancement or personal enrichment. The ways in which people gain new knowledge also begin to shift; adults come to rely more heavily on sources other than formal classes to learn what they need. Work experiences, job-related training programs, recreational activities, mentors and colleagues, and reading become primary sources of new knowledge. The mode of learning also typically changes. Instructor-dependent experiences give way to a greater number of self-directed or nonformal events.

Much has been written about the special characteristics and needs of the adult learner. Theorists and researchers such as Knowles (1978), Knox (1977), Kidd (1973), and other professionals who study and work with adult learners seem to agree to four principles for adult learning, as discussed below.

Principle One: Adults Need Relevant Learning Experiences. This means that adults want to be able to apply what they are learning to problems in their personal or professional lives.

An interesting series of studies that confirms the importance of content relevance was reported by Rogers, McCormick, and Krisak (1986).

They presented statistics instruction to nurses using their own nursing content area as the context for examples and problems (adaptive) or other content areas (nonadaptive strategies). That is, while some of these nursing students in the study received nursing-related content, others received less relevant content such as education or sports in their problems. These researchers found that those who received the adaptive treatments learned more than students who were in the nonadaptive treatments.

In what ways can the methods of computer-based instruction be made more relevant to adults? Appropriate use of screen display features of the computer is one way. For example, redundant graphics that work well for children quickly become tedious to adults. The density of information on a screen should be carefully planned. Too much or too little information on the screen is annoying. Student responses should be meaningful and not trivial. High-lighting techniques can be used to increase efficiency by reducing reading time. A mixture of media is usually preferable to a single medium.

Principle Two: Adults Have Rich Reservoirs of Experience Which They Want to Bring to Bear on New Learning. Adults do not come to an educational experience carte blanche. They are not content to passively accept viewpoints that do not fit with their own perceptions.

Sophisticated computer-management systems can better facilitate learner's own experiences and prior knowledge than can simple linear programs. Several approaches involve collecting learner profiles prior to instruction. Information about professional area, aptitudes, prior knowledge, and learning styles are examples of student data that can be collected. Students might then receive different instructional paths, depending on their profile scores. McCombs and McDaniels (1981, 1983) sought to determine whether they could develop individualized computer-based instruction through an empirical process. Air Force trainees completed a battery of aptitude and personality tests. Using stepwise multiple regression analyses, these researchers determined which of the student characteristics assessed were the best predictors of success in training modules where there was a wide range of performance. Based on these correlations, alternative treatments were defined for different lessons.

Certain types of computer-based instructional formats may accommodate an adult learner's experience base more than others. For example, a case problem or simulation that resembles situations found in daily life may be easier to relate to than one that is too far removed from reality. Tapping into a communications network such as a bulletin board that allows discussion of issues among colleagues may be a far more effective technique than a didactic approach, even if it takes more time.

Principle Three: Adults Want Interactive Learning Experiences. Not content to be passive, adults want opportunities to discuss, challenge, debate, and receive feedback on their ideas and progress.

In a traditional classroom setting, there are many opportunities for interaction between teacher and student, and student and student. One of the potential liabilities of newer technology-based formats is too much isolationism in the learning process. Johnson and Johnson (1985) warn that individualistic learning by computers can (1) promote social isolationism, (2) deny users opportunities to summarize orally and explain what they are learning, (3) prevent social modeling, (4) reduce valuable reinforcement from peers, and (5) work against natural preferences for working cooperatively. Nonformal learning experiences will be strengthened to the degree that students can interact with others as part of the experience, even if this interaction is totally technology based.

Informal instructional sequences must allow for thorough and frequent feedback to prevent learning errors and discouragement on the part of learners. Carrier and Sales (1987) found that when given the choice to see different levels of feedback irrespective of learning styles, all adult subjects requested the maximum amount of feedback available when responding to practice items in a computer-based tutorial. Systems that allow students to interact with an instructor and/or other students will reduce the problem of isolationism and enhance other feedback strategies.

Principle Four: Adults Want to Have Input into the Nature and Method of Their Learning Experiences. As experienced students, many adults feel they know how they learn best.

One of the most important implications of this principle is the need for access. Adults must be able to conveniently access both the hardware and software needed for the tasks they wish to accomplish. Busy adults must be able to fit the use of the technology in and around jobs, parenting, errands, and other responsibilities.

Another implication that relates to access is the ease of use of both equipment and programs. Communications software that automatically dials up frequently used data bases or electronic services is an excellent example of how the technical workings of software can be made transparent to the user. Easy-to-use spelling and grammar checkers make word processing a more efficient task.

Another aspect of self-direction is making decisions within the instructional sequence itself. This might occur, for example, when the user asks to skip ahead or to select more difficult problems or to determine the path to follow. Research on learner control suggests that some form of "coaching" in computer-based instruction (CBI) is better than simply giving learners total freedom about how much instruction they will receive and in what order (Hanafin, 1984).

It is especially crucial that learning experiences outside the classroom be motivating to the individual. Keller (1983) proposes that for instruction to be motivating, it must arouse and sustain attention, be perceived as relevant, inspire confidence that it is possible to succeed, and promote satisfaction about the expected outcomes of the task. These characteristics of motivating instruction take on even more importance when there is reduced guidance by live instructors.

Computers and Continuing Education

Heerman (1984) describes three ways in which computers may be used in continuing education. First, they can serve as teaching machines, presenting new material or providing practice and reinforcement. Second, they can be used as learning tools to promote the formation of new ideas, for instance through the use of word processing or spread sheets. Third, they can be used as learning resources to access information, as in the case of computer networks for communication with colleagues.

Examples from the continuing medical education field illustrate the benefits of computers for instructional purposes. Mozes (1982) describes the formulation of computer-based patient management problems at Michael Reese Hospital and Medical Center in Chicago. These simulations are designed to foster clinical skills and problem-solving processes needed in diagnosis and therapy. These programs can be distributed through networks so that physicians and other health care professionals can work on them at the office or at home.

Intelligent computer-assisted instruction (ICAI) systems apply principles of artificial intelligence (AI). Roberts (1985) describes AI as an attempt to have computers perform tasks that, if performed by human beings, would generally be considered to require intelligence.

He describes the expertise module as one that imparts knowledge and teaches how to use that knowledge. The student module makes hypotheses and points out misconceptions and inappropriate strategies. The tutoring module helps students select problems and prompts, criticizes, and monitors responses and selects remedial materials for the student. For instance, the program MYCIN is an expert problem-solving program for diagnosing myocardial infractions. The logic used in the program has also been used for other content areas. The strength of ICAI systems lies in the power they wield in analyzing heuristic approaches in problem solving and providing corrective strategies for optimizing performance. They maximize the benefits of one-to-one instruction by a tutor geared toward making the student aware of his or her higher-order thinking processes.

ICAI is in its infancy, but has much potential for instruction delivered outside the classroom in medicine as well as many other fields. Unfortunately, due to high costs of producing ICAI, its use is not widespread. The problems of limited vocabulary and syntax constrain the use of such systems, which is one of the major obstacles in their development and use.

Correspondence courses can also make good use of computer technology. Bender (1985) from the University of Mississippi has incorporated microcomputers as a way to personalize a correspondence course that is taken by 150 correspondence students and more than 300 on-campus students. Microcomputer networks are also used at the University of Kentucky to help business teachers gain computer-related skills under the guidance of university faculty. This program has provided teachers with instructional support through a network and thus allowed them to work on assignments at their leisure (Simpson, 1985).

Computers and Training in Business

The costs of education for corporations are staggering. Eurich (1985) reports that a conservative estimate for direct educational costs (not including employees' compensation figures for training time) runs to $40 billion annually and involves nearly 8 million students. IBM alone estimates that it now spends nearly $700 million annually on educational costs for its employees.

Increasingly, business is looking to technology for a solution to large-scale training needs. Many examples exist for how computers and related technologies are being used to speed up training, to make it more flexible, and to reduce costs associated with travel and time away from the job. One of the more state-of-the-art examples of using technological solutions for training is the recently constituted National Technological University (NTU). Satellite transmission will beam engineering courses designed at a variety of universities around the country, and students will be able to take these courses at their leisure. Students can earn a master of science degree in a variety of engineering specialties.

Digital Equipment's Interactive Video Information System (IVIS) integrates a variety of modalities—including text, voice, motion, graphics, and audio—into an adaptive system that uses learning styles as a basis for adapting to different needs. (See the chapter by Johnson, this volume.) Xerox Corporation uses a prototype adaptive testing system to pretest students for basic sales training. Students complete a self-instructional tutorial before they take sales training courses at a central training facility. Another tutorial is intended for service representatives focusing on service-call management, machine installation procedures, technical updates, and field problems. Another course instructs retail store employees in how to demonstrate equipment sold in Xerox stores.

Similar training programs are used in the Customer Service Division of Eastman Kodak Company to provide service technicians with equipment in troubleshooting. Simulations provide hands-on experience in replacing faulty equipment. At NCR, CAI courses include teaching how to program in BASIC, how to diagnose and repair computer printers, and (through the use of simulations) international business management skills (Thomasson and Larsen, 1986).

Wilson Learning Corporation's Interactive Technology Group has produced an interactive videodisc called "The Versatile Organization" that provides a computerized social style inventory score for each user. The individual can then observe examples of the implications of his or her own social style for interactions between salespersons and clients. This product is meant to be used in individualized settings such as learning resource centers in corporations. Its design is fast paced, upbeat, and highly interactive.

After reviewing methods used in corporate training settings, Eurich (1985) concludes that much instruction still occurs in traditional modes such as the lecture class. However, much experimentation occurs with different methods including widespread use of computer-based and computer-managed instruction.

Computers as Writing Tools

Computers are a boon to both competent writers and those in need of writing help. Word processing facilitates the preparation of documents for many purposes, from completing an assignment to writing letters to friends. The benefits of word processing are many. Andrews (1985) argues that the computer fosters a different mentality toward writing by emphasizing the process not the product. The computer allows for easy revisions, which encourages the writer to perfect rather than live with inadequacies in a document. Because the keyboard is faster than the pen, writing becomes less fatiguing, which may in turn encourage the writer to spend more time on the process. Other writing aids, such as spelling and grammar checks, reduce some of the mechanics to a more manageable level. Because word-processed drafts are easier to read than handwritten ones, it is easier to get feedback from others about one's writing. Packages that will restructure reference entries to meet format requirements for different style manuals simplify the process of organizing a bibliography.

Individuals in need of remedial writing training can also profit from existing software packages. Marchesano (1986) describes an example of such a package. This program, called Mach, is designed to reinforce basic paragraph skills. The initial stages of the program present a tutorial on focus, topic sentences, and concluding sentences. The student is then given an opportunity to see worked examples with practice questions. In the second part of the program, students are encouraged to write an original paragraph, using a structured dialogue with the computer. This program acts as a tutor and adviser in the writing process, detecting errors and programs that could be used by an individual without direct intervention from an instructor.

Computers and the Disabled

Several computer enhancements that permit wide access to educational resources have been developed for learners with disabilities. For example, voice recognition systems help students who cannot type but can vocalize sounds. Such systems enable computers to interpret different sounds as words or phrases. The person then makes the sound and the communication appears on the screen.

For people with visual impairments, there is access technology, which endows the computer with synthetic speech, enables the output to be produced in large print on the screen and from the printer, and produces output in braille. An example of special word processing software is called BEX, produced by Raised Dot Computing of Madison, Wisconsin. BEX will drive the echo speech synthesizer for the Apple computer. It will produce variously sized print on the screen. In addition, it will translate the original input into braille and drive several different braille printers.

Rogers, a professor of liberal arts at the University of Notre Dame, speaks highly of the "Talking Apple," which has helped him write despite a visual impairment (Rogers, McCormick, and Krisak, 1986). He uses an Echo Speech synthesizer with the Apple microcomputer. The voice constantly spells out what is typed, calling attention to errors that can be corrected. The computer voice is easily understood and can be lowered or raised to suit the user.

For students with impaired hearing, modems can be used to communicate with others, with or without hearing impairments, over the phone. Also, an electronic device called the cochlear implant includes a receiver over the ear. Sounds that it picks up are processed by a small computer carried by the person. The computer translates these sounds into electrical signals, which it sends back to the cochlear and then to the nerve cells. These devices are increasingly used by adults who are deaf.

About 6 percent of the U.S. population suffers from some form of learning disability, often manifested in difficulty in reading, spelling, and punctuation. Word processing programs, with their capacity to identify misspelled words, mistakes in punctuation, and grammar errors, should reduce the impact of these disabilities on the production of documents.

Potentials and Limitations of Computers for Learning in Nonformal Settings

Earlier sections of this chapter have emphasized new and exciting applications of computers and related technologies for learning in nonformal settings in a variety of contexts, such as continuing education or business. Because of space limitations, only a few of the more pervasive applications have been mentioned in this chapter. Increasingly, as the quality of software programs improves, as telecommunications technology develops, and as costs of computers and related technology decrease, many dramatic applications will emerge. With so much promise, it is also important to examine critical issues that suggest some caution in future efforts. Four such issues are addressed below in the form of need statements.

1. *There is a need to provide access to technology and technology-related products.* The widespread use of technology for learning is possible only if individuals have access to it at home, at work, or in the community. As the costs of technologies drop, computers should become as commonplace in the home as dishwashers and microwave ovens. But since this level of infusion is still years away, many students will need to use hardware and software outside their homes. Creating opportunities for convenient, flexible, and inexpensive access to this technology is an essential task for organizations that plan to deliver technology-based instruction.

Related to the issue of access is the continuing problem of the incompatibility of computer systems. Software that runs on one system may not run on a different system. An instructor who uses MS DOS materials may find that many of his or her students have access to systems that use different operating systems, such PRO DOS. Differing memory capacities of computer systems can also be a problem. A program requiring 256K will not run on a system with a smaller memory. Instructors will need to keep these software specifications in mind when planning instructional activities.

2. *There is a need to develop competence and comfort with technology.* Having a luxury car parked in the garage is of little use to the owner if he or she is afraid to drive. The same reasoning applies to the use of technology. State-of-the-art computer systems with impressive communications devices and peripherals are of little use if a student cannot operate them or is uncomfortable around them.

The use of technology for learning carries with it the added burden of ensuring that students are competent in the use of the media. Students will not have access to the substance of their learning activities if they do not have the skills for simple operations such as booting programs, saving information, or calling up data bases.

There are several ways to minimize this problem. First, the operating environment can be made as user friendly as possible. Many programs are now so easy to run that little if any prior experience with computers is necessary. A second approach is to provide direct instruction on using the technology. Such training is currently provided through many sources, such as vendors, employers, or community education courses. Many adults will learn on their own as they acquire equipment at home or at work. In nonformal settings, there will need to be opportunities for learners to determine if they need direct instruction on using hardware and software. If so, such learners may need assistance in locating resources that can provide the training.

3. *There is a need to carefully select learning experiences that can best be delivered through technology.* Most educators agree that while technology can be used to deliver instruction and information, there is a danger that it will be used inappropriately. An overused but excellent example of misuses is that of employing the computer to simply turn pages. Having

the computer present page after page of text is a misuse, because off-line printed materials are cheaper to produce and more portable.

Designers of nonformal educational experiences must be prepared to analyze the best mix of media, methods, and materials for students. Computers are effective at simulating, animation, querying learners, and storing responses. Off-line text materials are appropriate when large amounts of material must be presented. Live presenters (instructors) are highly effective when the modeling of attitudes and values is the goal of education. In planning instruction to be delivered outside of formal classroom settings, the importance of making each component optimally effective is amplified because instructor intervention may be reduced.

4. *There is a need for more high-quality software in critical areas.* The development of software is time consuming and costly, resulting in expensive final products. Marketing of software products is made difficult because of the incompatibility of systems. For these reasons, locating high-quality software to use in education, especially in some content areas, is a problem.

As discussed above, effective software draws on the capabilities of the computer and related technology in optimal and appropriate ways. It uses graphics, sound, and text in interesting ways. It can monitor and adapt to an individual's response patterns. It opens up new domains of information through data bases and other forms of telecommunications. Effective software for adults is easy to use and does not "talk down" to them in language or approach.

Software selection is made easier through groups like the Educational Products Information Exchange and Microsoft, who publish evaluations of software. Many professional journals now carry software reviews as well. Over time, the scope of such reviews will expand so that a greater variety of materials related to adult learning topics will be assessed.

Final Comments

In his book *Discovering the Future*, Barker (1985) describes "paradigm pioneers" as those individuals who recognize the need to switch from the prevailing paradigm in a field to new ones that promise solutions to formerly unsolved problems. In the area of adult learning experiences, that shift has begun. Technology allows for instruction to be delivered and received nearly anywhere at any time of the day or night. Such power at their fingertips should encourage educators to move toward planning instructional sequences for adults that employ the best features and capabilities of these new technologies.

References

Andrews, D. C. "Writer's Slump and Revision Schemes: Effects of Computers on the Composing Process." *Collegiate Microcomputer*, 1985, *3* (4), 313-316.

Barker, J. A. *Discovering the Future*. St. Paul, Minn.: ILI Press, 1985.
Bender, K. R. "Using the Computer to Personalize a Computer Course." *T.H.E. Journal*, 1985, *12* (7), 89-91.
Carrier, C., and Sales, G. "Pair Versus Individual Work in the Acquisition of Concepts in a Computer-Based Instructional Lesson." *Journal of Computer-Based Instruction*, 1987, *14* (1), 11-17.
Eurich, N. P. *Corporate Classrooms: The Learning Business*. Princeton, N.J.: Carnegie Foundation for the Advancement of Teaching, 1985.
Hanafin, M. "Guidelines for Using Locus of Instructional Control in the Design of Computer-Assisted Instruction." *Journal of Instructional Development*, 1984, *7* (3), 6-10.
Heerman, B. "Computer-Assisted Adult Learning and the Community College Response." In D. A. Dellow and L. H. Poole (eds.), *Microcomputer Applications in Administration and Instruction*. New Directions for Community Colleges, no. 47. San Francisco: Jossey-Bass, 1984.
Johnson, D. W., and Johnson, R. T. "Computer-Assisted Cooperative Learning." Unpublished manuscript, University of Minnesota, 1985.
Keller, J. M. "Motivational Design of Instruction." In C. Reigeluth (ed.), *Instructional Design Theories and Models*. Hillsdale, N.J.: Erlbaum, 1983.
Kidd, J. R. *How Adults Learn*. New York: Association Press, 1973.
Knowles, M. S. *The Adult Learner: A Neglected Species*. Houston: Gulf Publishing, 1978.
Knox, A. B. *Adult Development and Learning: A Handbook on Individual Growth and Competence in the Adult Years*. San Francisco: Jossey-Bass, 1977.
McCombs, B. L., and McDaniels, M. A. "On the Design of Adaptive Treatments for Individualized Instruction." *Educational Psychologist*, 1981, *16* (1), 11-22.
McCombs, B. L., and McDaniels, M. A. "Individualizing Through Treatment Matching Is a Necessary but Not Sufficient Approach." *Educational Communications and Technology Journal*, 1983, *31*, 213-225.
Marchesano, L. "Process CAI: A Bridge Between Theory and Practice in Writing Instruction." *Collegiate Microcomputing*, 1986, *4* (1), 83-87.
Mozes, G. "Professional Education and the Microcomputer." In D. G. Gueulette (ed.), *Microcomputers for Adult Learning: Potentials and Perils*. Chicago, Ill.: Follett, 1982.
Reinhold, F. "Macro Marketers." *Electronic Learning*, 1986, *6* (1), 30-36.
Roberts, F. C. "An Overview of Intelligent CAI Systems." *Peabody Journal of Education*, 1985, *62* (4), 40-51.
Rogers, S., McCormick, D., and Krisak, N. "Adapting the Thematic Context of Mathematical Problems to Student Interests: Individualized Versus Group-Based Instruction." *Journal of Educational Research*, 1986, *79* (4), 245-252.
Simpson, K. "Collegiate Instruction via a Microcomputer Telenetwork." *Journal of Business Education*, 1985, *60* (7), 280-282.
Sokoloff, M. "Linking the New Technologies with Special Education." *Media and Methods*, 1985, *21* (7), 13-16.
Thomasson, J. E., and Larsen, R. E. "The Personal Computer as a Vehicle for Learning in the Workplace." In B. Heerman (ed.), *Personal Computers and the Adult Learner*. New Directions in Continuing Education, no. 29. San Francisco: Jossey-Bass, 1986.
Zemke, R. "Evaluating Computer-Assisted Instruction: The Good, the Bad, and the Why." *Training*, 1984, *21* (5), 22-47.

*Carol A. Carrier is associate professor and assistant dean,
College of Education, University of Minnesota at Minneapolis.*

Learning outside the classroom may, in the future, be influenced by the emergence of new forms of integrated information technologies.

Using Integrated Information Technologies for Out-of-Classroom Learning

Dennis D. Gooler

Defining Information Technologies

The most common description of information technology involves a combination of telecommunications and computers, particularly microcomputers, with the capacity to make available to many users almost anywhere vast amounts of information. Cleveland (1985), for example, argues that the marriage of computers and telecommunications is the central event of this era, requiring a whole new conception of the idea of leadership. Glossbrenner (1983) observes that the owner of a personal computer is but a few steps away from entering an expanding universe of incredible size and power. Turkle (1984) suggests that the new technologies, especially the computer, catalyze change not only in what people do, but how they think. McCorduck (1985, p. 38) argues that a new "technology of the intellect" will change processes of every kind, from manufacturing to management, from design to agriculture, from scholarship to (perhaps) citizenship.

Many writers tend to be long on description of what information technologies can or will do and somewhat short on precise definitions for information technology. Hawkridge (1983) supplies one of the most complete definitions.

For the purposes of this chapter, information technologies might be descibed as having at least the following characteristics:
1. They offer a combination of computers, video, and telecommunications technologies in some integrated form.
2. They are capable of moving all kinds of information to users virtually anywhere in the world.
3. They make *more* information available *faster* than any past technologies.
4. The power of these technologies may bring about fundamental changes in our lives.

It is evident that integrated information technologies are more than simply computers, or television, or radio, or any other single medium that may have been used in the past for learning outside the classroom. Precise definitions of these technologies do not come easily, in part because the technologies themselves tend to be evolving at a rapid rate. Definition may best be served by example. In the next section of this chapter, a description of one particular information technology is offered.

The Education Utility: An Example of an Integrated Information Technology

The Education Utility is an information technology system being developed by National Information Utilities Corporation. The chairman of that company was instrumental in founding the Source, billed as the first information utility in the world. The Source provided access for thousands of users to a wide array of information resources. The Education Utility is, in some respects, a considerable elaboration of the concept of the Source.

The Education Utility system consists of four basic parts. The first part might be thought of as a gigantic information reservoir (physically stored and managed in a large central computer). That reservoir consists of many kinds of information, including (but not limited to) textbook materials, computer software programs of every kind imaginable, data bases, news services, reference materials, learning plans and programs, word processing programs, spreadsheets, newspapers, and journals— almost any information in any form can be digitized and stored in a computer. This reservoir could contain whole courses of study in philosophy, agriculture economics, automobile repair, English as a Second Language, stamp collecting, or virtually any other topic.

Three points concerning this information reservoir should be highlighted: First, because the Education Utility is designed to be an open system and user driven, what is actually in the information reservoir is a function of what the user of the system *wants* available. All kinds of people will be able to develop information resources to put into the system, and any user will have access to any or all the information in the system.

Second, the material in the reservoir can and will be continuously updated and expanded. That is, all the information in the reservoir should be current. News services, for example, will be current to the moment. Textbooks can be updated on a regular basis and the changes made available to all users all the time. Software programs can be tried out, revised, and put back into the system. Time-sensitive materials can always be maintained current. Because information itself is dynamic, the information storage or reservoir must also be dynamic, capable of responding to changes and additions to the world's information resources.

Third, the Education Utility will very shortly include motion video, which will permit individual users to have access to video and film resources.

At the moment, the information already contracted for storage in and distribution through the Education Utility National Coordination Center is small in amount but growing rapidly. The technology to handle the storage, preparation, and coordination of information resources in the reservoir is complete. As more and more users hook into the Education Utility, the amount and kinds of information resources available through the system will expand to meet the needs of users.

The intent of the Education Utility is to make these information resources available on demand to individual users. This requires that the information stored in the National Coordination Center be transmitted to the location of the user. The transmission technology represents the second crucial component of the Education Utility system. Put most simply, the Education Utility system will use whatever transmission sources are available and least costly to get materials to a user. In some cases, the transmission will be via telephone. As the system grows, however, it is likely that satellites will be the most widely used transmissiom channels.

One of the more significant aspects of the transmission element of the Education Utility system is the use of what is being called "real-enough" time. During the evening hours, much of the capacity of telecommunication systems is unused. Information from the National Coordination Center will be moved during these off hours, when capacity is high and costs are low. As a result, the Education Utility can offer low-cost service to users by taking advantage of the idea that most users do not need information on the spur of the moment but can plan for using information resources the next day or the next week, permitting movement of those resources during evening hours and thus saving enormous telecommunications costs. Some pundits have already labeled this process "moon mail"!

Another key to the economic success of the Education Utility is that the telecommunications channels needed to move information through the Education Utility system for the most part already exist. That is, the Education Utility does not require a massive effort to build an entirely new telecommunications system but rather will utilize telecommunications systems already in place.

The third component of the Education Utility system consists of a means of receiving from the main information reservoir, and subsequently storing at the local level, information required by users at that local level. This device has been labeled the "education resource computer." The device is capable of storing great amounts of information resources, directing those resources to the proper user at the proper time, metering usage of the information, and preventing software piracy. One basic assumption of the architecture of the Education Utility is that of storing as much useful information as close to the ultimate user as possible. The education resource computer, housed in a school building, a community library, a factory, or any other local facility becomes the focal point for information moving to and from local users. The education resource computer acts as an electronic mailbox for all local users. The resource computer makes it possible for individuals to call in by telephone to the information resources from their homes or offices. And, of course, the education resource computer allows users to bypass the costs of communicating on line with the national coordination center.

The education resource computer thus permits information to be stored close to the user. But how is such information kept current? Each night, revisions or additions to the main information resources reservoir are monitored. If information stored at the local level, in the education resource computer, is among those resources revised, updated, or otherwise changed at the national coordination center, a signal is automatically sent from the national center, updating relevant information resources being stored at the local level. Users, of course, will be notified of any such changes that have occurred.

The fourth piece of the Education Utility system is the individual work station, the place where the user actually makes contact with the Educational Utility system. Contact occurs through a microcomputer terminal, using whatever attached peripherals (such as printers, video equipment, and so on), the local setting or user has decided are necessary. Each work station will have enormous computing power in and of itself, but the power and flexibility of that work station is immeasurably greater than that of a stand alone microcomputer, because the work station has access to the full range of updated information resources available in the Educational Utility system. In addition to these information resources, of course, users will have at their fingertips all forms of productivity tools that will permit them to do interesting and important things with the information resources they now are able to access.

This discussion provides a cursory overview of the major components of the Education Utility system: (1) a National Coordination Center, which serves as the reservoir of information resources and gateways; (2) telecommunications channels (or electronic highways) along which the information resources will flow from the coordination center to the user and back; (3) the education resource computer, which acts as the local storage facility for information resources and as the critical "traffic cop" to move information to its intended user; and (4) the individual work station, where the user actually connects with and into the Education Utility system. The technology system is designed to be as transparent to the user as possible, but behind the friendly face of the technology is a complex system. (See Gooler, 1986, for further discussion of the system.)

Potential Benefits

The most obvious benefit from using integrated information technologies, such as the Education Utility, is that users will gain access to a tremendous amount and variety of information resources far beyond what is normally available to learners studying outside formal classrooms (or even inside most classrooms). The constraints on learning that are generally imposed by the availability of learning resources will be sharply reduced. To the extent that having access to more current information resources contributes to greater learning gains, students using information technologies should be greatly enriched.

The benefit here is more than simply having access to *more* information, for more is not necessarily better. What is impressive about the new information technologies is their capacity to present to the learner information resources of many kinds or from many sources and to enable the learner to integrate those various forms of information into learning programs that make sense. The learner is not restricted to just textbooks, video, or educational software. Furthermore, the learner need not even be confined to one form of video input but can use satellite-delivered television, laser discs, cable television, video recorders, and so on.

Of course, there is always a danger that learners or teachers will end up using this enormous information base in very unimaginative ways that do not capitalize on the potential learning power of the technology. But the potential for creative and dynamic uses of information is well beyond what has been available before.

A somewhat less obvious but nonetheless important benefit that could come from using information technologies is that each learner will be able to explore a number of learning modalities or strategies and ascertain patterns of learning that seem to work best. That is, the information technology systems that are emerging permit complex monitoring of learner performance, leading to more powerful diagnostic procedures to help plot what learners learn and do not learn and how they go about learning. Over time, it might be possible to match a particular learner's most effective approach to learning with certain characteristics of instructional materials and/or programs, making it more likely that hoped-for instructional outcomes will actually occur. There are some exciting developments occurring in this area whereby learner characteristics are matched with identified characteristics of instructional resources and, with the aid of error analysis packages, learners are able to select instructional materials and strategies that best suit their styles, use those materials in a planned instructional program, receive assistance in diagnosing specific learning difficulties that may have come about as the learner progresses through the instructional program and, when appropriate, receive instructional remediation designed to overcome these learning difficulties. These exciting prospects are not likely to be resident in most information technologies when those technologies are first implemented, but the technological capacity to handle this kind of instructional customization seems to be (at least theoretically) present. What remains is for educators and researchers to try various ways of building information about learning styles and strategies into the system itself. It is in such areas that expert systems may well hold promise.

A third benefit for those using information technologies is that participants involved in learning activities outside the classroom will be able to establish a learning community through the electronic mail and conferencing capabilities of the technology. Learners will be able to link up with other learners who are pursuing similar courses of study. Learners can develop ties with subject matter specialists anywhere in the world and come (at least electronically) face to face with some of the best minds in a given area. User groups are likely to form, giving learners a chance to interact on an ongoing basis with people of like interests. Joint learning projects can be undertaken. The possibilities are exciting indeed.

Too often, individualized education is thought to be synonymous with isolated education. The new information technologies, while permitting a true individualization of learning programs, will not require that learners be isolated in those individualized programs. Properly used, information technologies promote cooperative learning activities. This may be a particularly attractive feature to learners who cannot avail themselves of the socializing environment of a formal classroom but who wish nonetheless to have the opportunity to interact with other learners and teachers. The concept of a learning society where people engage in learning and interaction throughout their lives may become much more of a possibility through these new learning technologies.

Another benefit available through information technologies is the potential for making learning activities truly fun and exciting. Some would argue that this is of interest only to those involved with teaching and learning in traditional classrooms where motivation and interest are often problematic. Out-of-classroom learners, on the contrary, are already motivated, as evidenced by the fact that they are engaged in learning outside the classroom. There is some truth to this observation, but the truth of the observation does not negate the argument that learning through information technologies may be a lot of fun, primarily because learners have access to such a wide variety of information resources and because the technology will permit learners to do much with these resources. The motivating and captivating aspects of information technologies ought not be underestimated.

These are but a few of the direct benefits that might accrue to learners involved with information technologies. There are numerous other benefits that have been identified by those advocating uses of such technologies. Costs, for example, can be lowered significantly because of the volume of users that can hook into the system. Developers of software and other instructional materials will be stimulated to design material for these information technology systems, providing that the systems provide (1) a marketing highway to reach significant numbers of users, (2) an antipiracy feature that will make it impossible for users to inappropriately copy programs that developers have spent resources to create, and (3) the financial support to develop high-quality educational materials.

As teachers, learners, administrators, and others have started to find out about the possible uses and benefits of information technologies for out-of-classroom learning, enthusiasm has begun to build. There is caution, of course, because technological innovations in the past have tended to promise much more than was ever delivered. New information technologies appear to have great promise, but they also raise some important questions.

Issues in the Use of Information Technologies

As might be expected, there are many enthusiasts for the use of the new information technologies. But not everyone shares either the vision of, or the enthusiasm for, a society so heavily influenced by information and information technologies, as recent works by two authors indicate.

Winner (1986, p. 117) poses some fundamental concerns about the role and impact of emerging information technologies:

> Computerization resembles other vast, but largely unconscious, experiments in modern social and technological history. . . . Following a step-by-step process of instrumental improvements, societies create new institutions, new patterns of behavior, new sensibilities, new contexts for the exercise of power. Calling such changes "revolutionary," we tacitly

acknowledge that these are matters that require reflection, possibly even strong public action to ensure that the outcomes are desirable. But the occasions for reflection, debate, and public choice are extremely rare indeed. The important decisions are left in private hands inspired by narrowly focused economic motives. While many recognize that these decisions have profound consequences for our common life, few seem prepared to own up to that fact. Some observers forecast that "the computer revolution" will eventually be guided by new wonders in artificial intelligence. Its present course is influenced by something much more familiar: the absent mind.

Another writer who has introduced similar fundamental concerns with even more of a focus on information technologies and education is Roszak (1986, p. vii), who comments on the new information technologies:

No technology has ever unfolded its potentialities as swiftly as computers and telecommunications are doing. . . . Information technology has the obvious capacity to concentrate political power, to create new forms of social obfuscation and domination. The less prepared we feel to question the uses to which it is put, the more certain we are to suffer those liabilities.

These selected observations of Winner and Roszak provide a backdrop against which more specific issues about information technologies and learning outside the classroom might be considered. These crucial issues include the following:

1. Will the new information technologies create further problems of equity within our society? That is, will access to information technologies in general, and for learning outside the classroom more specifically, be limited only to the rich, to those who can afford to purchase expensive hardware or time on the system? Will urban centers provide opportunities for learners to use information technologies, while adults in rural areas are left with no access to this vast repertoire of information? Will there be gender differences in the use of information technologies? These questions of equity are of fundamental importance, for if only the "haves" can participate in learning through information technologies, then the social, economic, and cultural gaps in our society will widen even further, with potentially devastating consequences.

2. Who will decide what information resources will be made available through information technologies? Who will control what kinds of information learners are able to access? Will this become a kind of political tool to be used by individuals or agencies as a means of domination?

3. Let us assume for the moment that information technologies are accessible to virtually all citizens and that issues of equity and control are largely solvable. First, where will the needed kinds of *quality* information resources come from? There is much concern about the quality of existing instructional materials, particularly educational software. Further, the bulk of education materials that exist are directed primarily at in-classroom use or for use by children. Second, since most learning outside the classroom involves adults, where will the good information resources for use by those adults come from? And finally, how will information resources development be funded?

4. Can information technologies respond effectively to differences in learning styles and strategies among adults outside the classroom? How does one design an instructional delivery system that can accommodate these differences yet remain administratively manageable? Can information technologies actually deliver the enormous numbers and kinds of information resources that will be needed by populations outside the classroom?

5. How are issues of obsolescence of hardware, maintenance of hardware, installation, and so forth to be handled when attempting to deliver instruction outside the classroom to thousands of individual learners who are geographically scattered and who have differing levels of sophistication with respect to handling technology hardware? Will information technology facilities need to be restricted to certain locations, such as schools or libraries, or is it feasible to envision large numbers of people connecting to the information technology at their homes?

These are but a few of the important issues that must be addressed before information technologies are likely to enjoy widespread use in learning outside of classroom environments. Issues to be raised are of a philosophical as well as operational nature. The claims for information technologies are unlikely to be realized, or even adequately tested, unless and until some of these basic issues are addressed.

Conclusion

The new information technologies—combining computers, telecommunications, and video technology—unquestionably represent a whole new generation of learning tools. The claims made on behalf of these technologies are bold, grandiose, and exciting. The accuracy and realism of some of those claims have been questioned by those who are unconvinced or skeptical of the technologies. There are numerous and fundamental questions about the potential consequences of these technologies for society in general, and for individual learners in particular. Most experts seem to agree, however, that the new information technologies are different in some dramatic ways from previous technologies used for instruction and learning purposes.

For those interested in promoting and enhancing learning outside the classroom, investigations into the uses of new information technologies seem mandatory. What is required now is to move beyond the claims and the rhetoric, to begin to establish a base of experience with the new technologies. Educators need to experiment with a variety of approaches to using these technologies, to carefully evaluate the processes and results of such usage, and to report those results widely.

Educators have rightfully developed a certain level of cynicism about new technology "fixes." At some point, however, it seems appropriate for those interested in teaching and learning, including those whose interest is primarily in the teaching and learning that occurs outside the classroom, to grasp the opportunities to influence the design of new technology systems, and to make those systems work for learners, rather than to require learners to adapt to the requirements of technology. Because of the characteristics of emerging information technology systems, particularly those based on a more open design, opportunities for users to influence the shape of the technology may be available. Educators and learners might want to seize the initiative to influence the design and implementation of this next generation of information technologies, while simultaneously conducting the kinds of studies that will further an understanding of what it means to use those technologies.

References

Cleveland, H. *The Knowledge Executive: Leadership in an Information Society.* New York: Truman Talley Books/E. P. Dutton, 1985.
Glossbrenner, A. *The Complete Handbook of Personal Computer Communications.* New York: St. Martin's Press, 1983.
Gooler, D. *The Educational Utility: The Power to Revitalize Education and Society.* Englewood Cliffs, N.J.: Educational Technology Publications, 1986.
Hawkridge, D. *New Information Technology in Education.* Baltimore, Md.: Johns Hopkins University Press, 1983.
McCorduck, P. *The Universal Machine: Confessions of a Technological Optimist.* New York: McGraw-Hill, 1985.
Roszak, T. *The Cult of Information: The Folklore of Computers and the True Art of Thinking.* New York: Pantheon Books, 1986.
Turkle, S. *The Second Self: Computers and the Human Spirit.* New York: Simon & Schuster, 1984.
Winner, L. *The Whale and the Reactor: A Search for Limits in an Age of High Technology.* Chicago: University of Chicago Press, 1986.

Dennis D. Gooler is professor of education, Northern Illinois University.

Technology can facilitate instruction through presentation of content, monitoring of progress, and provision of feedback to learners.

Technology and Instructional Functions

Daniel D. Pratt

This chapter begins where a volume of New Directions for Teaching and Learning (Knapper, 1982) left off five years ago. A recurring theme of that sourcebook was the belief that the most important questions about the use of instructional technology are educational, not technical. That belief will be consistently stressed thoughout this chapter.

Technology is defined here as any means, form, or vehicle by which instruction is formatted, stored, and delivered to learners (Schwen, 1977). The context for discussing technology will be that of distance education, because it is from researching distance education that much current knowledge has been derived regarding technology and its place within education and learning.

Providing education seems to be dependent on two phases of activity: (1) the design, development, physical production, and storage of instructional materials; and (2) the bringing of learners into contact with materials and resources relevant to their program (Kaufman, 1986). Within each phase, educators are engaged in several instructional functions that ultimately influence learning. This chapter is about three of those functions and how they can be influenced by technology: (1) presenting content, (2) monitoring progress, and (3) providing feedback.

Instructional functions are not merely instructional tasks or activities

J. A. Niemi, D. D. Gooler (eds.). *Technologies for Learning Outside the Classroom.*
New Directions for Continuing Education, no. 34. San Francisco: Jossey-Bass, Summer 1987.

nor are they instructional roles, although there is a relationship between each of these elements. Functions are manifest in activities and tasks but start with a sense of purpose and a clarity of intention, for instance, knowing what to do and why it should be done. Intentions and a sense of purpose derive from a prior set of assumptions and beliefs regarding the nature of knowledge, the purpose of education, and the relationship between learner and teacher within the instructional process.

Presenting Content

For many, this function constitutes the essence of teaching, that is, the provision of information or the demonstration of skills. The functional goal or intent is to make available to the learner the content that will be needed for completing course objectives. An examination of most uses of technology in education reveals a dominance of this function over other instructional functions. Educators have, by and large, used technology to deliver content.

Some have been quite critical of this trend, noting that in many instances, the use of technology to deliver instruction has resulted in a polished product that often positions the learner as a passive recipient and presents knowledge as residing outside the learner. Information is packaged by "experts" for delivery to and consumption by learners. As Law and Sissons (1985, p. 47) note in quoting Davison (1975, p. 24):

> The people who experience exciting and immensely demanding learning tasks are the course teams. They are acquiring and organizing knowledge, evaluating and selecting materials, designing and presenting programs and activities. The student receives what appears to be a polished product from this process; he has to learn from material that has been agonized over by many others. In reality, the home-based learner receives at home; he thinks in markets, offices, workshops, pews, angling clubs.

Fortunately, several authors and a few institutions are moving away from this teacher-centered, exclusively didactic form of presenting content toward a more interactive and learner-centered use of technology to serve this instructional function. In virtually all cases, print is an important source of information and, as such, is considered an integral part of this instructional function.

Print Media. Baath (1979) has summarized the work of seven authors, ranging from B. F. Skinner to Carl Rogers, and reviewed each for its potential contribution to distance education. Most of the principles examined or ultimately derived are appropriate for any teaching-learning situation. What makes this sourcebook unique is that each principle is ultimately judged on its ability to contribute to our understanding of, or shape the practice of, distance education. As such, it is useful for anyone considering the use of technology in education because it examines traditional and contemporary means of providing distance education in terms of principles of learning and teaching.

Holmberg (1982) takes a different approach in reviewing research on distance education pertinent to course development. He summarizes findings and recommendations regarding the impact of text structure, lucidity and intelligibility, and use of grammar on text readability. In addition, he summarizes research on the density or compactness of text and the effect of inserted questions on "deep-learning." He also presents a brief summary of guidelines and sources of information regarding the use of graphics, including print size, clarity versus typographical elegance, and integration of texts and pictures. From his review, it is clear that presenting information through printed text or other mediated forms requires careful attention to a number of design factors, each of which can result in loss of student attention, misunderstanding, and/or decline in learning. (A comprehensive bibliography listing works on most aspects of graphics in texts is available from the Institute of Educational Technology of the Open University. In addition, the journal of *Instructional Science* devoted a complete issue to graphic communication [1979, *8* (3)].)

Waller (1979) and MacDonald-Ross (1979), starting from the assumption that learners read selectively, have developed instructional design strategies based on "access structures" that rely on the coordinated use of typographic signals, or cues, that help readers intentionally move around text selectively as they read.

Drawing heavily on the work of Waller and MacDonald-Ross, Marland and Store (1982) have also critically reviewed previous work on the use of advance organizers, overviews, pretests, objectives, inserted questions, and the use of graphics and typographical cues—not just as a means of orienting learners within textual materials but also as a way of facilitating learner control over instructional materials. This has been one of the more recent challenges in the use of any technology, that is, attempting to place the learner in control of the technology and the presentation of content via that technology.

One form of this challenge within print has been to create an impression of conversation whereby learners have a chance to participate and contribute to the dialogue. Holmberg (1983) summarizes the available evidence on text elaboration and the ways in which text can facilitate internalized conversation. His own theory is one of "guided didactic conversation." This approach resembles a guided conversation between students and authors, simulated through the learner's interaction with the course materials and made real through written, telephone, or computer interaction with a tutor.

The following assumptions (Holmberg, 1982, p. 9) are the basis of this approach:

1. The stronger the characteristics of guided didactic conversation, the stronger the students' feelings of personal relationship with the supporting organization.

2. The stronger the students' feelings that the supporting organization is interested in making the study matter personally relevant, the greater their personal involvement.

3. The stronger the students' feelings of personal relation with the supporting organization and the study matter, the stronger the motivation and the more effective the learning.

Law and Sissons (1985) point out several ways in which learners can participate in and contribute to the dialogue. The instructional materials and interactive process must place the learner in an active rather than a passive role vis-à-vis the tutor and the instructional materials. Written materials, cassettes, and even interactive systems using computer-assisted learning must allow for student reaction and generation of ideas, issues, questions, and opinions. These must be flexible enough to give the learner control over them rather than their controlling the learner. The use of loose-leaf notebooks, log books, diaries, and so on in addition to textbooks, can give the learner a greater measure of control over the materials. The positioning of physical breaks, attention-getters, marginal symbols, and white space can encourage students to generate as well as respond to issues and questions of importance.

However, one area of concern not reviewed by any of the above authors is the effects that may result from transferring information from one form to another. Each medium or technology may be likened to a culture that has its unique language and norms. Information originated in one form can never be quite the same in another form. Shakespeare in German is not quite Shakespeare; the plot is there, but the essence of Shakespeare is undeniably changed. Tennyson and Breuer (1984) call this "transmediation"—the transfer of information from its original form into a different form for instructional presentation. Whether this transfer involves a change from text to some other media (such as audiocassette) or from one form of prose to another that incorporates an "access structure," as discussed by Waller (1979), it implies a potential change in meaning. Content originally encoded in one form may be significantly changed if packaged in another form.

The transmediation process has relevance for notetaking as well. The work of Gallagher (1975; 1977) and Kern (1977) has shown that most students are quite capable of taking notes from radio broadcasts but find it impossible to take notes from television programs primarily because content delivered via radio uses the same verbal coding system as used in writing notes. Taking notes from television is quite different and requires encoding visual images (iconic and abstract symbols) with written verbal symbols, which sometimes results in a serious loss of information.

Nonprint Media. Not all students bring with them the necessary skills to learn effectively from a given technology, whether it is "new," as are computers, or "old," as is radio. The basic assumption is that learners' previous experience with a technology, and their subsequent expectations and attitudes toward that technology, may interact with the properties (unique or common) of a medium to affect the use of the technology and interpretation of the information carried. This phenomenological position regarding learning is well established and assumes a reciprocal effect between stimulus (situation) and learner. For example, work by Salomon (1981), Ksobiech (1976), and Merrill (1984) has shown that learners' beliefs about the demands placed on them by different media influences learning independently of instructional program features (Clark and Salomon, 1986).

Therefore, changes in this function are, in part, based on the belief that each time technology is involved in the delivery of education (that is, comes between the learner and the skill or knowledge desired), there is an interactive effect between the use of technology and the prior experience of the learner. This necessitates a clarification of the intended role for the technology within the instructional process. Two lines of research buttress this position. The first is concerned with unique properties and potentials of a given technology, and the second is concerned with the prior experience of the learner.

Properties and Potential. It is clear from a great many "comparison" studies that each technology cannot be treated as a unitary medium with absolute qualities that generalize across learners and situations such as television, radio, or computers (Clark and Salomon, 1986). Yet there is still the question of whether each medium is the potential for activating different mental operations. This line of enquiry has been of particular interest with regard to television (see Salomon, 1979; Salomon, 1983; Salomon and Cohen, 1977) and computers (see Papert, 1980; Pea and Kurland, 1985; Tikomirov, 1974). For example, Papert discusses the unique ability of computers to assist in developing metathinking skills (that is, learning to think about thinking). Yet, Zimler and Keenan (1983) found that children blind from birth performed as well as sighted children on tasks that were thought to require imagery input. This suggests that individuals may be capable of performing cognitive crossovers by processing information in ways quite different from the initial form of symbolic representation. Thus, the defining properties of a medium in and of themselves may not be crucial factors in eliciting unique forms of cognition.

Prior Experience. The most likely variable to affect a learner's constuction of information is his or her prior experience related to that presentation, that is, the content and technology used in its conveyance. Bates

(1982, p. 39), in reporting on the use of television to present case study materials for students, reported that

> The functions of the programmes in terms of the skills required of students, and the way content was treated, were quite different from those of the correspondence texts. The correspondence texts were theoretical, analytical, and didactic. The television programmes dealt with concrete situations, presented "images" of the complex, real-world situations, and were open-ended, open to interpretations, and non-analytical. Producers and academics expected students to analyze the television material, using the theoretical or analytical constructs provided in the correspondence texts; to apply what they had learned in the texts to the real-world situations observed in the television programmes; to generalize or draw conclusions from the specific instances in the programmes; to test, evaluate, or compare the applicability of general principles in the text to the "real-world" instances found in the television programmes.

Obviously, the producers and writers (as well as the tutors) intended that television should serve a unique instructional purpose, complementary to the role and function of print materials. The design of the written texts and the development of the television programs were undertaken with these complementary functions in mind. Yet, fewer than one-third of the students understood the purpose of such programs and appeared able to use the program material in the ways suggested. Another third of the students understood the purpose of such programs but appeared unable to use them in the intended way. Furthermore, a majority of learners wanted more help in using such programs.

Learners come to most forms of instructional technology, particularly radio and television, with a vast amount of experience. It is not surprising, then, to discover that their prior experience with such media affects their subsequent learning through those media. Again, the Open University provides some interesting evidence. Brown (1980) carried out a study of new students' attitudes toward radio and their subsequent use of radio as part of a foundations course. Although he found marked differences in students' listening habits, he concluded that their day-to-day use of radio had been poor preparation for their use of radio as a learning resource. For example, when asked whether they ever listened to the radio without doing something else at the same time, over half said they *never* listened to the radio without doing something else. This hardly represents the preferred use of a medium for instruction and learning!

Orienting Learners to Technology. It is becoming more and more apparent that there exists an important relationship between what a medium can do, what the educator wants it to do, and how it will be perceived by the learner. Those charged with the responsibility of designing and delivering information to be presented via instructional technology must not only have due regard for the characteristics of a medium and the prior experience of the learner but must also make explicitly clear the role and function of a medium in the educational process. Assuming that many learners have used technology in ways that may be counterproductive to its intended uses, these learners must be advised of the role and function of each form of technology used in their education before they start studying, that is, given an explanation as to why a particular technology is being used and how they are to use it in their learning. This applies for all instructional functions.

Monitoring Progress

Monitoring means the tracking of a student's progress on learning goals and tasks; it is both a formal and an informal function. Formally, progress is monitored through tests, worksheets, assignments, projects, and so on. In this sense, it is planned and systematic and might be seen as a part of evaluation. In an ad hoc sense, monitoring involves listening, observing, and interacting with learners and looking for indications of confusion, misunderstanding, or error in performance (gathering data). This function derives from a concern for the relevance and appropriateness of work assigned. The instructor's task is to make sense of performance data and to formulate a response, that is, to present more content or to provide feedback.

Two kinds of monitoring are relevant to our focus: reactive and proactive. Reactive monitoring starts with the assumption that learners are relatively self-directing and will initiate contact with a tutor when they need to discuss the content or process of their learning. Such a posture may also assume that to be other than reactive in monitoring someone's learning may constitute an unwarranted intrusion and may disrupt a natural process of enquiry and learning. Proactive monitoring begins with the assumption that it is in the learners' best interest for tutors to observe their work, to look for patterns that may be indicative of problems, and to initiate contact when necessary.

Interactive (usually computer-based) instructional systems are ideally suited to this function. For example, computer systems in Sweden, England, and America have been used to correct learners' responses, select relevant comments, and then provide feedback. In some cases (such as the CADE system in Sweden) the computer also checks and refers to the individual's earlier work when constructing a response. Mistakes are given appropriate comments, according to earlier work and with consideration for the nature of the current error. Such a system can be based on the use of multiple-choice questions constructed so that an error has identifiable distractors that cue up relevant explanations. Even correct answers are responded to when, based on a review of the learner's prior work, it seems important to emphasize crucial concepts or to support the need for continuing motivation. Instruction is based on cognitive principles of learning (Tennyson and Breuer, 1984) and is put into operation as computer-programmed decision rules, not the prearranged branching of its forerunner, programmed instruction.

An evaluation of one such system found that computer-assisted versions lead to better completion rates than tutor-marked versions of the same courses and also favorably influence students' attitudes toward the work (Baath and Mansson, 1977). Similar work in the United States is described in Brittain (1973).

Another advantage, as cited by Holmberg (1982), is that with the use of computers, tutors are less likely to misunderstand their role and, consequently, balance their time between presenting more information and monitoring and guiding students' enquiries.

Monitoring becomes particularly important when it is possible to make the right operation, or even provide the right answer for the wrong reason, as illustrated by Holmberg (1982, p. 18).

> Anyone who believes that .3 x .3 makes .9 (instead of .09) and that .2 x .2 makes .4 (instead of .04) will no doubt, on the basis of a false understanding, come to the conclusion that .3 x .5 = .15, which happens to be correct. . . . It is evident that the operation is not enough; we must pay attention to the knowledge and understanding on which it is based.

In summarizing three evaluation studies of computer-assisted learning (CAL) at the Open University, Scanlon and others (1982, p. 62-63) describe how one such system (Merlin) worked:

> After calling up the tutorial they wish to study . . . students are asked to type their answers to these profile questions. These answers enable the computer to draw up a profile of each student and route that student through the tutorial most appropriate to his or her ability. Each tutorial starts by establishing a question and answer dialogue which is aimed at improving the . . . complex concepts with which the student showed a weakness in the profile questions.

This particular system of CAL not only does an initial diagnosis on each student but also has a human tutor available for interaction.

The human tutor is situated at the telephone switch board associated with the computer, and watches a visual display screen which shows the progress of all the students currently using the computer tutorial program. By typing a suitable command, the display can be made to provide a detailed analysis of any student's answers and to pinpoint his or her "weak" concepts. If, at any time, a student types the word help or if either the Merlin program or the tutor decides that a student is doing particularly badly, then the student will be put into direct voice contact with the tutor. . . . With the help of the visual display . . . the tutor can provide personal assistance of a type which no computer program can supply. At the conclusion of the conversation the student can automatically continue the computer tutorial precisely where he or she left off.

Ironically, however, the use of such sophisticated systems to monitor and diagnose learners' work may actually counter other important factors necessary to continuance and learning. In Scanlon and others' (1982, p. 69) evaluation of the supervised mode of the program Merlin, the replies to questionnaires indicated that

The majority had no preference for either supervised or unsupervised tutorials. Of those who stated a preference, 66 percent preferred the *unsupervised* [emphasis mine] mode, but of these 66 percent only 33 percent had actually tried the supervised mode. Those who preferred the supervised had tried both.

According to Scanlon and others (1982, p. 69), comments on the supervised mode included the following:
- Students thought the tutor [might] assess them
- The tutor came on the telephone line too soon before the student had time to think the problem through
- Tutors could not isolate the student's problem
- Students were shy of talking to the tutor
- Students were afraid of being thought stupid.

In contrast, a few advantages of the supervised mode were also expressed, namely, students thought the tutor saved them time in sorting out a problem. Yet there is a question of just how students were perceiving the supervised mode of monitoring and diagnosis via computer and tutor. It may be that this function needs to be performed with the greatest of concern and caution so as not to violate any other advantages of learning through technology that may be important motives for the learner's enrollment and continuance, such as wanting to study within the privacy of one's home, at one's own pace, and with the expectation that the technology will continue to have infinite "patience" with initial learning, even through trial and error. The supervised mode, as operationalized in Merlin, may contravene some of the expected benefits and, in so doing, reduce a learner's willingness to use its most crucial feature, the ability to monitor and adapt to each individual learner.

Whether reactive or proactive, successful monitoring requires that educators recognize the multiplicity of functions they serve and the interdependent nature of those functions. Monitoring, for example, serves no purpose if the instructor never acts on data gathered. Monitoring is essentially the gathering of data related to learners' progress and needs so that further assistance may be provided.

Providing Feedback

Feedback is defined here as any message following a response made by the learner and the giving of information related to the learner's progress with goals, tasks, or effort. As a tutorial function, feedback serves three purposes: First, to provide learners with knowledge of results (with success of their efforts at learning); second, to provide information related to correcting or extending their work; and third, to provide support or encouragement based on effort as well as accomplishment.

Knowledge of Results. Feedback that is specific to knowledge of results has almost a century of research documenting its necessary place in learning. Out of that research have come two principles that are unquestioningly accepted and sometimes applied inappropriately through the use of technology. One is the principle of immediate confirmation of a correct response. Popularized in the 1960s, the principle suggests that the main function of feedback is to reinforce a correct response. Most readers will remember using programmed texts that provided comment following each "frame." Thus, whenever possible, a learner would be immediately reinforced after each correct response. This kind of feedback was considered essential to the shaping of a learner's response.

However, there is a convincing body of evidence to the contrary (Bardwell, 1981; Hartley and Lavell, 1978) that suggests the most efficient use of feedback is to provide information on incorrect responses, so that learners can locate and correct their errors. The former has been called "knowledge of results," and the latter "informational feedback."

Informational Feedback. The difference between knowledge of results and informational feedback can be seen in computer assisted learning. Anyone who has worked on a program that simply gave messages like CORRECT or ERROR, in response to each trial recognizes the inadequacies and disruptiveness of such a cryptic message, regardless of how immediately it followed the response. Such a message does not provide the learner with enough information. In fact, the CORRECT message alone has been shown to have no significant influence on some students' learning and to be dysfunctional to others. If the response is ERROR, the learner is left to wonder what to do to make it CORRECT. There is little real information in either message and, if received from a "live" teacher, such messages could be quite disconcerting.

A second principle concerning feedback has to do with the timing of the feedback. Technology has provided the means to give learners instant feedback on the appropriateness of each response, followed immediately by an explanation or supplementary information. This principle has been a hallmark of operant psychologists, who argue that initial learning is facilitated by immediate feedback and that once the behavior has been learned, delayed feedback facilitates further acquisition and retention of that learning. Yet, Gaynor (1981) and Bardwell (1981) found differential effects, with immediate feedback facilitating acquisition of knowledge-level objectives and end-of-session feedback facilitating comprehension and application-level learning. Further, they found that delayed feedback provided at the end of a session helps highly confident learners and facilitates their learning of more abstract and conceptual material that requires higher-order thinking. Apparently, anything that impedes the pace of these learners (such as constant interruptions to say CORRECT) is seen as dysfunctional. Conversely, immediate feedback was found to be beneficial for initial acquisition of knowledge for students having difficulty learning content.

Thus, feedback in the form of knowledge of results tells a learner when an error has occurred or when a response is correct. Informational feedback should tell a learner not only when a response is wrong but also provide information to help correct the error. Cohen (1985) and Roper (1977) give more detailed advice regarding when to use immediate versus delayed feedback and how to clearly and appropriately design end-of-session feedback. There is no evidence to suggest that these findings apply differently across media (that is, whether there is a difference between using on-line, computer-based and interactive systems, or printed texts).

Support. The last primary intent of feedback is to provide support and encouragement, reinforcing effort as well as achievement. This is a particularly crucial function when considering persistence and discontinuance of learners at a distance. Studies have shown rather conclusively that there is a distinct correlation between turnaround time (the time elapsing between students' dispatch of assignments completed and their return) and course completion (Holmberg, 1982). In addition, an Australian study has identified two variables of cognitive rather than circumstantial nature as being positively related to persistence: self-confidence and perceived support from significant others (Bowlay, 1979). Students with higher self-confidence and more perceived support tended to complete a first year; those with lower measures tended to discontinue.

It is here that either personal tutors or sophisticated interactive systems can provide necessary and sometimes essential support. Often students drop out when they think their tutor or the source of feedback is not helpful or does not care about them. Similarly, if comments are overly critical, a student's motivation to continue may be diminished. Any perception that the system, whether personal or technological, does not understand the difficulties a learner may be experiencing can have serious effects on the learner's motivation to continue.

This category of concern (namely, psychological support) is nicely dealt with in a manual produced by the Open Learning Institute of British Columbia (Rusnell, 1984). A variety of special need students are discussed, with recommendations for establishing rapport and providing assistance over the telephone. A special section is devoted to women students and issues such as lack of support from family members, exploration of employment options, unrealistic expectations of students en route to the work force, and women students trying to take more control of their lives. Each concern is dealt with as a part of providing feedback and support.

As with all tutorial functions, the use of feedback should not ignore known principles of learning or instruction. However, care should be taken when importing principles and instructional design strategies derived from significantly different audiences and circumstances. As educators move toward more complex and flexible uses of interactive systems that involve computers, videodiscs, and other high technology, they must be guided by sound educational principles and yet remain open to questioning the rules and guidelines governing instruction and learning that are borrowed from traditional classroom practice and print-based learning.

Conclusion

Obviously, there are no easy routes to effective instruction whether one uses technology or not. Indeed, there are no universally agreed-on definitions of what constitutes instructional effectiveness. However, when considering the use of technology within education, the effectiveness of instruction will depend on several interacting variables, including the nature of the content to be learned, the nature of the technology used, the time available, the cost of delivery, the quality of the learning experience, and the ability to respond to differences among learners. While circumstances might dictate priorities among these variables (cost), each of the three instructional functions examined illustrates a primary concern for the use of technology: the ability to respond to individual differences. It is here that technology may be able to make its most valuable contribution to education.

A basic question arises in the consideration of these tutorial functions: Should technology be considered only in terms of traditional teaching functions, or are there ways in which technology can significantly alter the nature of instruction and learning beyond the more traditional forms discussed here? Thus, a major question when considering any new technology in the delivery or provision of instruction must be, "What type of learning will it promote and how will that shape our thinking about instruction?" If educators continue to look in the "rear-view mirror" to understand each technology and its role in the provision of learning, they will only see it in terms of their prior experience. To forecast a future is not easy and may be more frustrating than fruitful. The best source of wisdom on the future use of technology to enhance learning, with or without the guidance of a tutor, may be the learners themselves. To understand the effects of a technology from the perspective of the learner is to allow a vast army of people to think about and experiment with that technology.

Finally, one form of technology is not inherently superior to any other form; the test of effectiveness lies not in the form but in the ability of a technology to serve specific instructional functions. Technology should do for learners what they cannot do for themselves. Conversely, technology should not do for learners that which they can do for themselves. Hence, educators should view technology through a template that seeks to make technology obedient to the needs of the learner and consonant with sound principles of instruction and learning.

References

Baath, J. A. *Correspondence Education in the Light of a Number of Contemporary Teaching Models.* Malmo, Sweden: Lieber Hermods, 1979.
Baath, J. A., and Mansson, N. O. *CADE—A System for Computer-Assisted Distance Education.* Malmo, Sweden: Lieber Hermods, 1977.
Bardwell, R. "Feedback: How Does It Function?" *Journal of Experimental Education,* 1981, *50,* 4-9.
Bates, A. "Learning from Audiovisual Media." In *Student Learning from Different Media in the Open University.* Institutional Research Review, no. 1. Milton Keynes, England: The Open University, 1982.
Bowlay, D. J. *Motivation and External Students: Pleasure or Profit?* Perth, England: A.S.P.E.S.A. Forum on External Studies, 1979.
Brittain, C. V. "Computer-Assisted Lesson Service at USAFI: An Interim Report." Paper presented at the annual meeting of the American Educational Research Association, New Orleans, 1973.
Brown, D. "New Students and Radio at the Open University." *Educational Broadcasting International,* 1980, *13* (1), 40-42.
Clark, R. E., and Salomon, G. "Media in Teaching." In M. Wittrock (ed.), *Handbook of Research on Teaching.* 3rd ed. New York: Macmillan, 1986.
Cohen, V. B. "A Reexamination of Feedback in Computer-Based Instruction: Implications for Instructional Design." *Educational Technology,* 1985, *25* (1), 33-37.

Davison, J. "Education Counseling in Academic Studies." *Teaching at a Distance.* 1975, *3*, 16-24.

Gallagher, M. "Decision-Making in the British Education System." Broadcast Evaluation Report, no. 2:E221. Milton Keynes, England: The Open University, 1975.

Gallagher, M. "Patterns of Inequality." Broadcast Evaluation Report, no. 22:D302. Milton Keynes, England: The Open University, 1977.

Gaynor, P. "The Effect of Feedback Delay on Retention of Computer-Based Mathematical Material." *Journal of Computer-Based Instruction,* 1981, *8,* 28-34.

Hartley, J. R., and Lavell, K. "The Psychological Principles Underlying the Design of Computer-Based Instructional Systems." In J. Hartley and I. Davies (eds.), *Contributions to an Educational Technology.* Vol. 2. London: Kogan-Page, 1978.

Holmberg, B. *Recent Research into Distance Education.* Hagen, West Germany: Zentrales Institut fur Fernstudienforschung, 1982.

Holmberg, B. "Guided Didactic Conversation in Distance Education." In D. Sewart (ed.), *Distance Education: International Perspectives.* London: Croom Helm, 1983.

Kaufman, D. "Computers in Distance Education." In I. Mugridge and D. Kaufman (eds.), *Distance Education in Canada.* London: Croom Helm, 1986.

Kern, L. *Student Feedback on Broadcast CMA Questions: An Interim Report on D204.* Milton Keynes, England: The Open University, 1977.

Knapper, C. K. "Technology and Teaching: Future Prospects." In C. K. Knapper (ed.), *Expanding Learning Through New Communications Technologies.* New Directions for Teaching and Learning, no. 9. San Francisco: Jossey-Bass, 1982.

Ksobiech, K. "The Importance of Perceived Task and Type of Presentation in Student Response to Instructional Television." *AV Communication Review,* 1976, *24* (4), 401-411.

Law, M., and Sissons, L. "The Challenge of Distance Education." In S. H. Rosenblum (ed.), *Involving Adults in the Educational Process.* New Directions for Continuing Education, no. 26. San Francisco: Jossey-Bass, 1985.

MacDonald-Ross, M. "Language in Texts." In L. S. Shulman (ed.), *Review of Research in Education.* Itasca, Ill.: Peacock, 1979.

Marland, P. W., and Store, R. E. "Some Instructional Strategies for Improved Learning from Distance Teaching Materials." *Distance Education,* 1982, *3* (1), 72-106.

Merrill, M. D. "Learner Control and Computer-Based Learning." In B. K. Bass and C. R. Dills (ed.), *Instructional Development: The State of the Art II.* Dubuque, Iowa: Kendall/Hunt, 1984.

Papert, S. *Mindstorms: Children, Computers, and Powerful Ideas.* New York: Basic Books, 1980.

Pea, R., and Kurland, M. "On the Cognitive Effects of Learning Computer Programming." *New Ideas in Psychology,* 1985, *12* (2), 37-68.

Pratt, D. D. "Tutoring Adults: Toward a Definition of Tutorial Role and Function in Adult Basic Education." *Adult Literacy and Basic Education,* 1983, *7* (3), 138-152.

Roper, W. J. "Feedback in Computer-Assisted Instruction." *Programmed Learning and Educational Technology,* 1977, *14,* 43-49.

Rusnell, D. *Tutor Orientation and Training Manual.* Richmond, B.C.: The Open Learning Institute, 1984.

Salomon, G. *Interaction of Media, Cognition, and Learning.* San Francisco: Jossey-Bass, 1979.

Salomon, G. *Communication and Education: Social and Psychological Interactions.* Newbury Park, Calif.: Sage, 1981.

Salomon, G. "The Differential Investment of Mental Effort in Learning from Different Sources." *Educational Psychologist,* 1983, *18,* 42-50.
Salomon, G., and Cohen, A. A. "Television Formats, Mastery of Mental Skills, and the Acquisition of Knowledge." *Journal of Educational Psychology,* 1977, *69* (5), 612-619.
Scanlon, E., Jones, A., O'Shea, T., Murphy, P., Whitelegg, L., and Vincent, T. "Computer Assisted Learning." In J. Martin (ed.), *Student Learning from Different Media in the Open University.* Institutional Research Review, no. 1. Milton Keynes, England: The Open University, 1982.
Schwen, T. "Professional Scholarship in Educational Technology: Criteria for Inquiry." *AV Communication Review,* 1977, *25,* 35-79.
Tennyson, R. D., and Breuer, K. "Cognitive-Based Design Guidelines for Using Video and Computer Technology in Course Development." In O. Zuber-Skerritt (ed.), *Video in Higher Education.* New York: Nicholos, 1984.
Tikomirov, O. K. "Man and Computer: The Impact of Computer Technology on the Development of Psychological Processes." In D. Olson (ed.), *Media and Symbols: The Forms of Expression, Communication, and Education.* 73rd Yearbook of the National Society for the Study of Education. Chicago: University of Chicago Press, 1974.
Waller, R. "Four Aspects of Graphic Communication." *Instructional Science,* 1979, *8* (3), 213-222.
Zimler, J., and Keenan, J. M. "Imagery in the Congenitally Blind: How Visual Are Visual Images?" *Journal of Experimental Psychology: Learning, Memory, and Cognition,* 1983, *9,* 269-282.

Daniel D. Pratt is professor of adult education, University of British Columbia.

Technological advance has engendered new approaches to instructional design and raised new design issues.

Instructional Design and New Technologies

Craig Locatis

This chapter is concerned with designing instruction for outside classrooms at locations where learning will occur at a distance from the teaching source. Some commonalities in distance education programs are identified, and technological developments affecting the future of distance education are described. Three approaches for designing distance instruction using new communications technologies are discussed, and general guidelines for designing distance instruction are presented. Although many of the chapter's concepts can apply to designing distance instruction in many contexts, most concern new technologies, especially those that are information based. While other chapters focus on specific information technologies, such as computers and interactive video, the approach here is more generic. An underlying theme is that new technologies and information tools are as likely to be subjects of study in many distance education programs as they are to be means for delivering instruction.

Commonalities

Distance education programs vary along the following common dimensions.

Use of Human Intermediaries and Technology. Either humans or technology can be a sole source, main source, or supplemental source of instruction in distance education programs. Generally, media have a key role and are chosen on the basis of their intrinsic capabilities to deliver content, accessibility to the target learner population, and cost. The number of learners exposed to instruction and the time frame within which content is expected to remain current are major factors in determining media use and technology's role. The roles of humans depend on their availability and their subject matter and teaching expertise. While human intermediaries are used mainly as teachers or tutors, they also can function as coaches, counselors, and advisers. For example, a real estate sales program distributed by a national association places brokers in teaching roles, requiring them to conduct group activities in their offices. But the program also requires new agents to take action after each lesson, often by seeking additional information and advice from more experienced agents, thus encouraging informal mentoring within a firm. In some cities, public librarians have been trained to interview patrons wanting education and to counsel them about relevant distance education courses.

Use of Individualized and Group Instruction. Distance education is not necessarily individualized, even when technology is involved. For example, a soft drink company distributes videocassette programs to bottlers who require managers to conduct formal group training at their plants. A computer company broadcasts seminars on artificual intelligence throughout the world that require groups to assemble at sites equipped to receive the transmissions. And when distance education *is* individualized, it does not have to be technology intensive. A telephone company, for example, distributes job aids and provides every supervisor with guides for explaining the aids to employees. Each person trained is given extra job aids and guides to teach others. This "each one teach one" approach with print materials is a viable way to train employees, especially those in rural areas where the teaching sites are usually the tailgates of the service trucks.

Centralization and Communication with the Instruction Source. Decentralized programs allowing little communication with the instruction source are one extreme; highly centralized programs with maximum communication are the other. The army develops technical extension courses centrally but uses them with troops at different posts who have little communication with course creators. The previously mentioned artificial intelligence seminars, on the other hand, are delivered from a central point and allow direct contact. Many programs mix decentralized instruction and communication with the information source. For example, a university operates a nationwide network of computer-based lessons that students can access remotely. The system has a computer mail messaging facility allowing instructors and students to send notes to each other.

Motivations for Developing Distance Education Programs. Generally, distance education programs are undertaken because more, better, or standardized instruction can be made available in this way than through conventional classes or courses or because more people can be taught for less by distance teaching. The real estate program described earlier was developed to make instruction available to employees of small firms unable to provide their own formal training. Computer and videodisc continuing education programs have been created to provide better instruction by allowing physicians to diagnose infrequently occurring illnesses in simulation. The army's technical courses described earlier were produced to ensure that every soldier receives identical training and to reduce costs of sending people to technical schools. The motivations for initiating distance education programs may effect success and almost certainly shape design and development efforts.

Technological Developments

Although communication and information technologies do not have to be used for distance education, there are compelling reasons for considering them, not the least of which is their prevalence in the culture. Several developments, some current, some pending, will make certain technologies more pervasive and increasingly attractive for delivering distance education. Some of these trends and innovations have been described in previous chapters, but a few are worth noting here.

More Channel Capacity. Cable television systems have thirty-five channels or more. Standard telephone lines have been converted to seven-channel capacity (Tatum, 1986). The use of satellites and fiber optic systems makes channel capacity almost unlimited. Moreover, band widths, or the amount of information that can be transmitted over a channel in a given time period, are increasing. The national newspaper, *USA Today*, can digitize a full newspaper page into 60 to 100 megabits, compress the data to 6 to 10 megabits, and send it by satellite at 150 kilobits per second to remote locations where it is reconstituted for printing.

Increased Storage Capacity. It is possible to store 54,000 still images or one-half hour of continuous motion in analog format on one side of a twelve-inch videodisc. Compact disks with read-only memory (CD ROMs) are capable of storing 540 million bytes of digital information, or roughly 150,000 text pages, 1,000 images, or one hour of high quality audio on one side of a four and three-quarter inch disk (Miller, 1986). Grollier distributes its encyclopedia on CD ROM and uses less than 20 percent of the space available. Other larger optical disks can store up to 1 billion bytes of information, and jukebox-like devices enable access to multiple videodiscs or compact disks without having to manually change platters. At present, commercially available videodiscs and optical disks are not erasable, updatable, or reusable, but such capabilities, are under development. Some current systems allow users to record information once only, although they can retrieve it many times.

Integrated Media Capabilities. New media tend to integrate older ones. Videodisc players, for example, can show single images much like slide projectors and motion sequences much like television or film. Presently, CD ROM disks can only have six minutes of motion, and the process is slow, jerky, and discontinuous. Recently, a standard has been announced for a CD/I, or compact disk interactive, that will present text, still images, continuous-motion images, and audio using a single disk and player (Lowe, 1986; Geest, Bruno, and Mizushima, forthcoming). The technology is under development and is supposed to be interfaced with existing CD ROM and videodisc devices. Thus, core instruction might be obtained from a CD/I player, but videodisc and CD ROM players also could be accessed to provide additional information.

Interlinked Information Systems. Networks allow independent and heretofore incompatible devices to be interconnected. Commercial systems such as TYMNET and TELENET link terminals and computers together by phone, allowing individuals access to different data bases, electronic mail, bulletin boards, shopping catalogs, and other services. Currently, migrating among different information systems is a problem. Users must log on and off each, and the systems themselves vary significantly in terms of protocols, commands, and arrangement of information. "Gateway" software is under development, allowing automatic log-on to more than one system. Information requests in the language of one system are automatically translated into that of the others to generate appropriate retrieval. Systems like the one described in Gooler's chapter in this book are being developed to use such software to make vast stores of multimedia materials available to the education community.

Faster Retrieval. Devices exist that can search free text at rates of up to 10 million characters per second for complex patterns of up to 10,000 characters. Massive amounts of information can be searched rapidly, and complex searches are possible.

These developments make it more feasible to (1) build knowledge bases containing primary information, such as actual documents, rather than bibliographic data bases referencing primary sources; (2) access more varied information electronically, including text, images, and audio; and (3) provide information technology users with more options to generate, exchange, and otherwise manipulate information.

Technological advance will likely increase the number and change the character of information options people have available. These advances will fuel existing efforts to publish more information electronically and to develop more intelligent and user-friendly software for managing information. More people are likely to be linked electronically, either at the home or office, in an environment that is more information dense, complex, and interactive.

These trends already are evident in the proliferation of microcomputers in homes, offices, and schools, in public library programs that loan computers or provide computer access, in private company and government agency efforts that provide public information services, and in programs that provide free, open access to community computer systems. The city of Cleveland's community computer, for example, will provide a "post office" (electronic mail), a "school" (data bases accessible to teachers, parents, and students), a "hospital" (data bases of health information and a facility allowing users to ask certified physicians medical questions), and a "public square" (electronic bulletin board) (Grunder, 1986a, 1986b).

New technologies are obvious mechanisms for delivering education at a distance. But they also provide people with new electronic tools (word processing software, spreadsheets, data-base management aids) as well as access to information systems people need to learn about. The technologies and tools are themselves subjects to be taught in distance education programs.

Instructional Designs for New Technologies

Distance education programs in the future should be designed to accommodate new technologies where appropriate. Design depends on the specific technologies employed, the technical and design knowledge of program developers, the software used for author instruction, and the funding available. Scenario-based instruction, hypermedia, and parallel systems are three generic instructional designs illustrating some learning environments that new technologies make possible.

Scenario-Based Instruction. These designs place learners in high fidelity "worlds" of video and graphic images. The worlds can be realistic or fantasy. Learners usually are given a goal and must perform tasks to achieve the goal. Learners usually have a wide range of choices available while interacting, and their performance is monitored in the background. Remedial instruction is provided either at the end of the scenario, if they fail to attain the goal, or during interaction, if too many errors are made. The interface makes interaction easy, often through the use of touch screens, voice recognition units, or other input devices.

Videodisc emergency simulations that hospitals subscribe to and receive monthly are examples of scenario-based instruction. The programs are used on special work stations having microcomputers, videodisc players, and touch-screen monitors. Physicians view video episodes of changing patient conditions over time. They gather information and prescribe therapies by touching selections on the screen. When the simulation is over, the physicians can repeat the experience, see an explanation of the case, compare their decisions to experts' decisions, view highly structured lessons explaining the condition portrayed, or access references (Allen, 1986). Another example is the army's STARS program (Reeves and others, 1982).

Soldiers play a video game where they have to travel back in time to give General Patton a message. To attain this goal, they must perform several computational and navigational tasks. They are automatically branched to remedial exercises when errors are made, and they must complete these successfully to resume play. The game is, in fact, a diagnostic basic skills test that is unintimidating, indeed invisible, to the learners.

Hypermedia. These designs provide learners with knowledge bases of information and tools for exploring them. The knowledge bases may be textual, graphic, pictorial, or some combination and can be independent or interlinked. Each display in the knowledge base functions as a "menu" to other displays, and contains cues to additional information available. Learners browse through or search the knowledge base or access other knowledge bases, using menus. They mark displays for later retrieval, for referencing personal notes, or for evoking searches. Hypermedia environments have been proposed where documents and images could be copied and modified by others to encourage joint authorship. A trail could be kept on these transfers to show the evolution of ideas and to pay original authors royalties for the use of their work (Nelson, 1983).

An example of hypermedia design is an electronic textbook in pathology (Thrush and Mabry, 1980). Terms in inverse video indicate availability of additional text or images. Pop-up menus are evoked by positioning the cursor on a term, and learners can opt to view images on videodisc, see definitions, or search for the term or related terms in the text. The idea is to eventually have an electronic bookshelf so that learners studying the pathology text might instantly jump to other textbooks for related information. A second example is an experimental program teaching pushcart assembly (Stone and Hutson, 1984). The initial menu is simply a graphic of the entire cart. Positioning the cursor on any part of the cart causes other displays of assembly diagrams and/or written directions to appear. A third example is a visual data base in anatomy (Bridgman, Telford, and Allen, 1985). Bar codes are embedded in a hardcopy textbook. A small computer with a wand-like bar code reader is used to zap up related images on videodisc by moving the wand over the bar codes. The computer then accesses visuals on the videodisc to augment those in the text. A visual data base with a different interface overlays icons on visuals, and learners can target these with the cursor, perhaps to see pictures at greater magnification or from different angles (Wertheim, 1986).

Parallel Systems. These designs involve constructing complementary teaching and testing programs around a common knowledge base. Users can access the knowledge base in either information, instruction, or test modes. In information mode, they browse or retrieve text and visuals related to topics of interest. In instruction mode, additional predesigned information and teaching strategies are provided. In test mode, questions are presented and knowledge assessed. The knowledge base, instructional strategies, and bank of topic test items exist as separate computer fields but are cross-indexed so that the user can start interacting in any mode and shift between modes at any time. Thus, one user might start exploring a topic in information mode, decide to be tested on it, and, depending on results, opt for instruction. Another user might choose to be tested on the contents of the entire knowledge base and then review only certain sections by looking up information or being taught.

This author has been unable to identify systems that have been designed intentionally for use in either tell me, teach me, or test me modes. One system, however, has some of these features. AI/Rheum is an expert system that diagnoses rheumatological conditions. Physicians and medical students can submit data for a new case or choose a case from the system's library. The system indicates whether or not it has sufficient information to render a diagnosis. When diagnoses are made, the program indicates which findings support them and what additional information would confirm the primary diagnosis or an alternative. Users can ask the system to display the rules used to reach a decision or have it tell or show them more about diseases or clinical findings. The system displays additional text or videodisc images in response to these requests (Kingsland, Lindberg, and Sharp, 1986). Moreover, a complementary system, AI/Learn, is being developed to teach the visual concepts needed to discriminate among the different clinical conditions depicted on the videodisc and to teach the rules for diagnostic reasoning.

The instructional designs described have the following common characteristics: They are information rich; they provide unprecedented amounts of learner control over what content will be learned and the sequence and pace of instruction; and they provide for fast interactions, almost in immediate response to learner requests. If these designs are indicative of others that might emerge, then the new information technologies make possible more open instructional environments that are intrinsically motivating and effective (Lepper and Malone, in press). In fact, sophisticated learners might do better using these designs than more structured and traditional ones (Snow and Lohman, 1984). But the designs are not for everyone and may not be possible or practical to implement in many circumstances.

Design Guidelines

Instructional development models and design strategies have been presented before but not necessarily for new information technology. The following general guidelines might be useful in designing distance education programs for these media. They are suggestive, not prescriptive, and augment those advanced for other media.

Use a Systematic Approach. Various systems models for developing instruction have been advanced. These vary, but most identify fundamental activities for creating instruction, such as assessing learning needs, identifying teaching goals, choosing media, designing lesson prototypes, conducting lesson try-outs, and making revisions (Andrews and Goodson, 1980). New technologies do not obviate the need for careful planning. Indeed, planning is more crucial, since the instructional environments can be complex. Distance instruction developers should adopt, adapt, or devise an appropriate development model that will provide a common framework for organizing development activities, discussing design issues, and assigning tasks and responsibilities.

Consider the Instructional Context. Who are the learners? Where are they located? Where will learning occur? These questions, crucial in designing all types of instruction, become paramount in distance education, where alternative means must be identified for linking instruction and learners and where disparities exist in learner access to technological resources. If new information technology is to be used for distance education, the target learner population must have access to it.

Determine the Roles of Human Intermediaries and Technology. Often human teachers are not available at learning sites or their subject and teaching expertise are too varied. In these situations, technology may dominate or support. Technology also can provide instructor access at a distance through the use of computer network message facilities or phones, which can help learners contact both instructors and each other. Thus, technology can expand, rather than suppress, the use of human teaching resources.

Incorporate Instructional Events. There are are certain factors or events that are known to affect learning. For example, people learn when they are given appropriate information, have the opportunity to practice, and receive performance feedback (Gagne, 1984, 1977). Unfortunately, teaching fundamentals seems to have been forgotten by some, especially when devising instruction for new technologies. Glitzy programs or dull programs often result that are both only marginally effective.

Be Imaginative. New technology can present instructional events in innovative ways (see MacLachlan, 1986), including the use of more adaptive and intelligent computing programs (see Sleeman and Brown, 1982). But old methods often get imported into new media, even when the value of some older methods is dubious. For example, some early videodisc programs were essentially lectures. And some lessons integrating videodiscs and computers look as though their computer and video components are separate programs. When computers and videodiscs are used together, the resulting learning environment is more than the sum of its parts, and designs should reflect this. The varied capabilities of new communications media need to be bonded.

Consider the Interface. There are devices that display computer and video images on a single screen and allow designers to overlay graphics on video. Touch screens, mice, and voice-recognition units can be used, although they are not always practical. But, even if the keyboard is employed, human factors concerning screen size, display legibility, and so forth should be taken into account (Shneiderman, 1980). Moreover, the interface should be "transparent" so that learners are less aware of technology as an intervening tool. Hammers exemplify this concept. Users automatically focus on the head and the object to be pounded, not the interface or grip (Rutkowski, 1982). The structure of the hammer itself is essentially transparent, or ignored by the user.

Provide Navigational Aids and Movement Devices. Information is stored electronically with new technology and is retrieved by moving, often nonlinearly, through various computer and video displays. The magnitude of the electronic environment usually is not apparent. For example, the size of a hard-copy book is known at a glance, but an electronic text is unfathomable. In addition, computer screens display less information than printed pages and are not as easy to flip through. Moreover, it is not as easy to find one's place in an electronic environment. Screen labels and special displays indicating where students are in a lesson should be provided (Kerr, 1986). It should be possible to page forward and backward through consecutive displays, move among lesson sections, exit a lesson, and return to the departure point (Carr, 1986). Learners should not be electronically constrained.

Embed Instruction into Applications Software. When applications software, such as a word processing program or retrieval system, is to be learned, the software and related instruction should use the same medium and form a common interface (Moran, 1981). For example, instruction on using a word processing program for a microcomputer should be accessible on line and made part of the word processing package. Although it may be appropriate to provide documentation such as manuals and additional instruction using some other media, students and user ideally should be able to access related instruction on the computer itself. Further, an effort should be made to reduce the amount of instruction required by including on-line help as part of the software and by making the software's prompts, menus, and commands easily understandable. Users should be able to exit the software at any time, access related instruction, and return to where they left off.

Embed Software into Instruction. Since the computer is a tool to accomplish intellectual tasks essential to certain content domains, it can be incorporated into educational programs. For example, word processing software might be part of a journalism course, and spreadsheets might be used to teach accounting. Using such software can promote computer literacy and alter learning dynamics. Students are more willing to revise term papers, for example, when they have word processors to ease the task (Lockheed and Mandinach, 1986). The design of instructional programs should take these factors into account.

Provide Documentation and Assistance. Some microcomputer lessons require two disk drives or extra software before they can be run. When computers and videodisc players are used together, player switches have to be set. Until new technologies become more standardized, program developers should provide good technical documentation and support.

Conclusion

Distance education programs are diverse and make varied uses of technology. The pervasiveness of new communication and information technologies is altering the environment in which distance education takes place. Distance education programs have been developed that use these new technologies, and their use will likely increase because of technological advances. The new technologies create new environments for learning and instructional design. However, most programs using new technologies fall into one of three categories: those that teach effectively but are dull, those that are imaginative but do not teach, and those that do not teach and that are not imaginative. There is, of course, a fourth category of programs that are both imaginative and effective. Commercially available programs fitting this category are rare. Some innovative, largely experimental designs have emerged that involve learner manipulation of complex and varied information forms. But designing for new technologies is only beginning to be understood. There are rules of thumb based on learning principles and experience that can help guide development efforts. Those guidelines presented here only touch on a host of provocative design problems and issues such as how and when to give learners instructional control (Tennyson, Christensen, and Park, 1984), the incidental and unprescribed learning that accrues from using information technology (Perkins, 1985), how attributions affect learning from technology (Saloman, 1984), technology's social-psychological affects (Turle, 1980), and the impact that authoring software can have on the design and use of interactive instruction (American Association of Medical Colleges, 1986). The instructional designs described here are as information-rich as our culture. Empowering people to understand and use information resources and technology is one of the major challenges confronting instructional designers and distance educators.

References

Allen, D. "DXter, the Clinical Simulator." Presentation at the meeting of the Consortium of IVIS Developers in the Health Sciences, DECDworld Conference and Exposition, Boston, February 1986.
American Association of Medical Colleges. *Medical Information in the Information Age: Proceedings of the Symposium on Medical Informatics.* Washington, D.C.: American Association of Medical Colleges, 1986.

Andrews, D., and Goodson, L. "A Comparative Analysis of Models of Instructional Design." *Journal of Instructional Development,* 1980, *3* (4), 2-15.
Bridgman, D., Telford, I., and Allen, F. "Advanced Communication Technologies Applied to the Design of Anatomy Learning Resources." Paper presented at the annual meeting of the American Association of Anatomists, Toronto, April 1985.
Carr, R. "New User Interfaces for CD ROM." In S. Lambert and S. Ropiequet (eds.), *CD ROM: The New Papyrus.* Redmond, Wash.: Microsoft Press, 1986.
Gagne, R. *The Conditions of Learning.* (3rd ed.). New York: Holt, Rinehart & Winston, 1977.
Gagne, R. "Learning Outcomes and Their Effects: Useful Categories of Human Performance." *American Psychologist,* 1984, *39* (4), 377-385.
Geest, D., Bruno, R., and Mizushima, M. *Standardization of CD-I.* The Netherlands: Phillips New Media Systems, forthcoming.
Grunder, T. "The Community Computer." Paper presented at the Working Conference on New Communications Technologies and Health Promotion, National Cancer Institute, Bethesda, Md., July 1986a.
Grunder, T. "Interactive Medical Telecomputing." *New England Journal of Medicine,* 1986b, *314,* 982-985.
Kerr, S. "Learning to Use Electronic Text: An Agenda for Research in Typography, Graphics, and Interpanel Navigation." *Information Design Journal,* 1986, *4* (3), 206-211.
Kingsland, L., Lindberg, D., and Sharp, G. "Anatomy of a Knowledge-Based Consultant System: AI/Rheum." *M. D. Computing,* 1986, *3* (5), 18-26.
Lepper, M., and Malone, T. "Intrinsic Motivation and Instructional Effectiveness in Computer-Based Education." In R. Snow and M. Farr (eds.), *Aptitude, Learning, and Instruction: III. Cognitive and Affective Process Analysis.* Hillsdale, N.J.: Erlbaum, in press.
Lockheed, M., and Mandinach, E. "Trends in Educational Computing: Decreasing Interest and the Changing Focus of Instruction." *Educational Researcher,* 1986, *15* (5), 21-26.
Lowe, L. "CD-I: Technology at the Focal Point." *Video Computing,* 1986, May/June, 14-17.
MacLachlan, J. "Psychologically Based Techniques for Improving Learning Within Computer-Based Tutorials." *Journal of Computer-Based Instruction,* 1986, *13* (3), 65-70.
Miller, D. "Finally It Works: Now It Must 'Play in Peoria.'" In S. Lambert and S. Ropiequet (eds.), *CD ROM: The New Papyrus.* Redmond, Wash.: Microsoft Press, 1986.
Moran, T. "An Applied Psychology of the User." *Computing Surveys,* 1981, *13* (1), 1-10.
Nelson, T. *Literary Machines.* Swathmore, Penn.: Ted Nelson, 1983.
Perkins, D. "The Fingertip Effect: How Information Processing Technology Shapes Thinking." *Educational Researcher,* 1985, *14* (7), 11-17.
Reeves, T., Aggen, W., and Held, T. "The Design, Development, and Evaluation of an Intelligent Videodisc Simulation to Teach Functional Literacy." In *Proceedings of the Fourth Annual Conference on Video Learning Systems.* Warrenton, Va.: Society for Applied Learning Technology, 1982.
Rutkowski, C. "An Introduction to the Human Applications Standard Interface." *Byte,* 1982, *7* (10), 291-306.
Saloman, G. "Television Is Easy and Print Is Tough: The Differential Investment of Mental Effort in Learning as a Function of Perceptions and Attributions." *Journal of Educational Psychology,* 1984, *76* (4), 647-658.

Shneiderman, B. *Software Psychology: Human Factors in Computer and Software Engineering.* Cambridge, Mass.: Winthrop, 1980.

Sleeman, D., and Brown, J. *Intelligent Tutoring Systems.* New York: Academic, 1982.

Snow, R., and Lohman, D. "Toward a Theory of Cognitive Aptitude for Learning from Instruction." *Journal of Educational Psychology,* 1984, *76* (3), 347-376.

Stone, D., and Hutson, B. "Computer-Based Job Aiding: Problem Solving at Work." Paper presented at the annual meeting of the American Educational Research Association, New Orleans, April 1984.

Tatum, R. "Project Victoria: The 7 in 1 Solution." *Telephone Engineer and Management,* 1986, *90* (1), 47-51.

Tennyson, R., Christensen, D., and Park, S. "The Minnesota Adaptive Instructional System: An Intelligent CBI System." *Journal of Computer-Based Instruction,* 1984, *11* (1), 2-13.

Thrush, D., and Mabry, F. "An Interactive Hypertext in Pathology." In *Proceedings of the Fourth Annual Symposium on Computer Applications in Medical Care.* New York: Institute of Electrical and Electronic Engineers, 1980.

Turle, S. "Computer as Rorschach." *Society,* 1980, *17* (2), 15-24.

Wertheim, S. "Computer-Assisted Learning Systems in Neuroanatomy." Paper presented at the LaserActive Conference and Exposition, Boston, October 1986.

Craig Locatis is training specialist, National Library of Medicine/National Institute of Health, Washington, D.C.

A variety of technologies is available for learning outside the classroom, offering a number of benefits, but raising some important issues as well.

Themes and Issues

John A. Niemi, Dennis D. Gooler

A review of the chapters in this sourcebook reveals a stunning array of technologies that are and might be used for learning outside the classroom. To be sure, technologies have been used to deliver out-of-classroom instruction for many years. In one sense, many of the technologies reviewed in this sourcebook are not new, although some have not been used extensively for learning outside the classroom. Several of the technologies discussed in the foregoing chapters, however, are relatively new and may represent a dramatic and even fundamental change in the kinds of technological delivery systems used to provide learners with access to educational opportunities outside the boundaries of formal classroom settings.

Debating whether a given technology is new or different, however, is a fruitless exercise. What is more important is to examine both the benefits ascribed to uses of the technologies and some issues raised by such uses, as described by the authors of these chapters.

Benefits of the Technologies

Each author has sought to identify some of the benefits to be derived from using a particular technology to enhance learning outside the classroom. While the cumulative list of benefits is quite long, it is possible to categorize or summarize those individual technology benefits into six broad categories.

J. A. Niemi, D. D. Gooler (eds.). *Technologies for Learning Outside the Classroom.*
New Directions for Continuing Education, no. 34. San Francisco: Jossey-Bass, Summer 1987.

Access to Learning Opportunities. One of the fundamental premises of learning outside the classroom is that such learning opportunities are more available to more people than would be possible were learning restricted to formal classroom settings. That is, access to learning opportunities is a crucial aspect of any discussion of learning outside the classroom.

Technology, it is argued, makes providing access to learning opportunities a reality for more and more diverse people. Broadcast television, as Wiesner points out, is an obvious example of a technology that expands access to learning opportunities. Takemoto describes the ubiquitous nature of radio and other audio technologies; she observes that with audio there is no longer any place that is "outside the classroom." As a technology, the print media have opened doors to learning for untold millions of people. Rapidly, computers and various forms of integrated information technologies are expanding access to learning opportunities to many who would not or could not avail themselves of learning experiences if restricted to the time and place of a classroom setting.

The implications of increasing access to learning opportunities for more and more people cannot be taken lightly. In many respects, it is argued, technology is making it possible to move closer to the idea of a true learning society, a goal continuing educators have long espoused and sought. To the extent that the next generations of individuals will live in a world increasingly dominated by need for and uses of information, and to the extent that learning is prerequisite to survival, to say nothing of prosperity, access to learning opportunities becomes a fundamental social issue. The authors of the chapters in this volume tend to argue that technologies are the key to expanding access to learning opportunities and thus that technologies are increasingly important to societal development and stability.

Access to More and Better Information Resources. A related benefit ascribed to technologies used for learning outside the classroom is that not only can technologies expand access to learning opportunities but information resources thus accessible to learners are greatly improved.

Johnson's example of the interactive video art experience is a vivid rendering of the kinds of learning that might be made available through technologies. Carrier's examples of the ways computers are being used in nonformal settings suggest learning experiences that go well beyond what has been known in the past. Gooler's description of integrated information technologies paints a picture of learners with virtually unlimited access to the world's information resources. Wiesner's perspective on the potential uses of video also suggests an incredible array of information resources and products available to learners for learning outside the classroom.

Futurists have long warned us about the coming of the information age, when the amount and kinds of information available in society will be almost overpowering. Most individuals can testify to this in their own lives. And yet, learners are often unduly constrained by their lack of access to relevant, current, and varied information resources. The technologies described in this volume speak of doing away with such constraints, of opening the world to every learner. There are, of course, serious concerns that accompany access to more and better information. Learners can get overloaded, lost in the maze of information. But they can also learn how to organize and use information to enhance their ability to achieve their learning goals. Their lives can be enriched by taking advantage of access to a broad range of information resources. More than ever before, the technologies available for learning outside the classroom make it possible for learners to gain entry into the wealth of the world's information resources.

Variety of Learning Strategies. Either explicitly or implicitly, most authors of the preceding chapters suggest that technologies make possible a variety of learning styles and strategies for those who engage in learning experiences outside the classroom. One of the benefits of technology use for out-of-classroom learning is that technology can address individual learning needs and styles, in large measure because technology offers opportunities for instruction to occur in ways other than a lock-step, traditional mode. Technology enables learners themselves to shape the learning modality. Pratt observes that the best source of wisdom on the future use of technology to enhance learning may be the learners themselves.

It is interesting to consider the variety of ways people can pursue learning objectives, given the existence of the kinds of technologies described in this sourcebook. Some people might learn some things best through participation in simulations of various kinds; computer technology, interactive video, and integrated technologies offer powerful simulation capabilities. Some people learn best through an audio medium. For still others, a visual experience through a video medium best addresses their learning preferences and styles. And, as Moore points out, print may be the medium of choice for many people.

The technologies now available for learning outside the classroom are of sufficient variety and quality that actually making alternative learning approaches available to learners is more feasible than ever before. Locatis provides examples of instructional designs that make possible instructional environments that are intrinsically motivating and effective. Educators have long subscribed to the rhetoric of individualizing education for each person, but they have not, in the past, found ways to make such individualization either accessible or manageable. The chapter authors in this volume urge educators to consider again the possibility of meeting the learning goals and styles of a wide variety of learners.

Increased Motivation to Learn. A closely related benefit ascribed to technology is that technology can motivate learning by providing a fun or interesting experience. The reader can sense a spirit of adventure and excitement in these authors' accounts of learning through technology. Again, Johnson's description of the art experience suggests an approach to a topic that is dynamic and exciting. Locatis writes about interlinked information systems, giving the reader an image of an intellectual journey of great interest. Carrier's mention of talking computers for visually impaired individuals raises a fascinating concept of learning that is both possible and stimulating. Gooler's discussion of the information utility hints at unleashing the human imagination through access to a range of new information resources. Numerous other examples could be cited.

Even when someone chooses, for whatever reason, to engage in learning outside the classroom, that learning is often not easy. To the extent that technologies can make learning more exciting, interesting, and meaningful, the motivation to engage in lifelong learning experiences will be increased. The technologies described in this volume offer possibilities for making learning even more interesting.

Individualized and Cooperative Learning. To some people, learning outside the classroom sounds like an isolated and isolating experience. Classroom settings often provide not only content but social interaction, a factor sought by many adults. Can technologies not only provide increased access to learning opportunities but do so in a way that is not totally isolating?

The technologies described in this sourcebook hold promise for not only being able to *individualize* learning opportunities, but for creating *cooperative* learning projects that do not necessarily isolate a learner. That is, to individualize should not be taken to mean to isolate. For example, Gooler and Locatis describe systems that enable us to learn to network or be connected electronically with others. And Takemoto mentions conferencing capacities through audio media.

The issue of personal contact, or interaction between teacher and learner or among learners, has been of considerable interest to those working with learning outside the classroom. The issue is both an instructional and social one and is raised by many authors in this sourcebook. The characteristics of the technologies presented here, however, appear to have potential for solving some of the isolation factors that have worried continuing educators. The capacity to achieve higher levels of interactivity, both as part of an instructional sequence and as an adjunct to instruction, is much greater with today's technology systems than has ever been true, even in the recent past. Such interactivity is not automatic, of course, but must be carefully planned and included in the application of the technology. However, it is encouraging to recognize that the ability to achieve much higher and more satisfying interactions among learners is here. It is almost an article of faith among the writers that such interactivity, and indeed possibilities for cooperative learning endeavors, will enhance learner performance and satisfaction.

These benefits of technology for out-of-classroom learning must be considered in the context of a number of issues raised by the authors. Again, each discussion of a specific technology contains descriptions of issues or problems, sometimes defined as limitations, accompanying the use of that particular technology. The following represents a summary of those overriding issues that apply to most of the technologies discussed.

Issues

Access and Equity. The technologies described in this volume are said to be capable of expanding access to learning opportunities well beyond the reach of formal classroom settings. The issue concerning access, however, is this: Given that technologies *can* expand access, *will* they? Or, more to the point, to whom will these technologies be accessible? What is of concern here is the matter of equity: Will technologies expand the gulf between those who have and those who have not?

To some extent, questions of equity are relevant to each of the technologies described. Print media, for example, are accessible only to those who can afford to buy printed materials, who have access to repositories of print materials, and who can read. Broadcast television is available only to those who can afford (or who have access to) television sets. Audio media, particularly radio, may come closest to providing universal access.

It is the newer technologies that present the greatest challenge of equity of access. Carrier, in discussing the uses of computers, raises the issue of access to relevant equipment. For many people, such technological conveniences as dishwashers and microwave ovens are not available, to say nothing of computers. Access to instruction via computers or through interactive video or integrated information technologies is limited in today's society; this creates an equity problem.

Quality of Materials and Programs. Technologies are perhaps best thought of as purveyors of content. Common to discussions of virtually all the technologies mentioned here is the issue of the quality of the materials or programs delivered via the technologies. In most cases, software production is costly. Much of what passes for information resources available in education is inferior. There is great concern among the authors about the existence (or absence) of adequate amounts of software or information products that can be delivered via the technology systems discussed. Until this critical issue is resolved, the available technologies limit the results that can be achieved.

Locatis addresses many of the information product design questions that are central to the development of quality educational materials. Johnson speaks to similar issues regarding interactive video. Pratt stresses the importance of well-designed instructional programming. Wiesner discusses the tensions involved in balancing production values, academic requirements, and costs. In each of these chapters, the concern is with quality and appropriate instructional materials.

Continuing educators have historically been concerned about the availability of good materials for learning outside the classroom. Some notable progress has been made on this issue, such as the work done at the Open University of the United Kingdom. But on balance, there is still a perception that inadequate amounts of high-quality, relevant materials exist.

Development Costs. Closely associated with the issue of the availability of quality materials are the issues of costs involved to develop good materials and of where funds to support such development may be found. Little more needs to be said about this issue, other than that it permeates discussions of technology applications in education.

Standardization and Obsolescence. Of concern to many of the authors are questions of hardware standardization and obsolescence. The hardware requirements involved in some of the technologies described are considerable and confusing. There is often incompatability within a kind of technology class, such as microcomputers, so that the purchase of one kind of hardware makes it impossible to use other kinds. This lack of standardization makes it very difficult for agencies or individuals to select hardware systems, and thus the technologies are not popularized as completely as might be desirable. People are afraid to commit scarce resources when there is a chance they will make the wrong choice and end up with technology they cannot use.

Similarly, there is concern about obsolescence; a piece of hardware or a system is purchased today, and tomorrow it is obsolete. There is considerable reluctance to invest in technologies for fear of premature obsolescence. Sadly, manufacturers have not always exercised much care in preventing obsolescence, and so the buyer must beware. Such an attitude does little to encourage widespread uses of technologies.

Human Contact and Interaction. One of the attributes of a number of the technologies described is their ability to increase the level of interactivity within educational programs and between learners. The other side of that attribute is a concern that technology is isolating, encouraging passivity on the part of the learner, and is unable to provide the human contact dimension so important to learning.

Technology-based learning systems have tried to address this problem in a number of ways. The Open University utilizes tutors to supplement the technology delivery system. Pratt discusses aspects of providing feedback as a form of support to the learner. Takemoto describes audio teleconferencing as one means of increasing interaction among learners.

Future responses to this issue will likely focus both on finding means for learners to interact in creative ways with other learners and with experts and on building more interesting and effective feedback systems within the technologies learners are using (as in the interactive nature of some of the video programs described by Johnson, the systems described by Gooler, and the computer applications mentioned by Carrier).

Training Users of Technology. An issue that underlies the application of all the technologies used in learning outside the classroom concerns the preparation of the learner to use the technology in question. Several authors comment on the need to train people to use technologies for learning. Learners cannot be expected to always know the best way to use a given technology to accomplish their learning objectives, nor is it always the case that each learner can readily learn how to use a technology on his or her own. Unless the learner is comfortable with a technology, there is little likelihood that he or she will be able to take full advantage of the technology.

It is easy to imagine that training is required only for the new technologies such as computers. However, there is some evidence to suggest that many learners are not comfortable in using more simple media such as audio technologies or even print.

If technology is to be effectively used for learning outside the classroom, careful thought must be given to how to prepare people to use such technologies. This kind of training might be accomplished in a variety of ways but definitely should not be overlooked. Locatis rightly notes that empowering people to understand and use information resources and technology is one of the major challenges confronting instructional designers and distance educators.

Conclusion

In this concluding chapter, the editors have attempted to identify some themes common to the discussions of technologies presented in this volume. Other issues, such as those concerning copyright, broadcast time, and so forth, are important to the long-range future of technology use for learning outside the classroom.

The best conclusion is probably a rereading of the ending of each of the chapters, for each author has provided a comment on the future prospects for and concerns about the technology analyzed.

Perhaps the material contained in this sourcebook will turn out to be another marker in the history of technological development, adding to our understanding in some measure, and making it more than likely that adult learners will capitalize on the benefits and minimize the ill effects of technology as they continue to learn outside the classroom.

John A. Niemi is professor of adult education, Northern Illinois University.

Dennis D. Gooler is professor of education, Northern Illinois University.

Index

A

Academy of Aeronautics, and interactive video, 37
Adult basic education, and television, 14
Adult education: computers in, 52-55; and experience, 53; interactivity in, 53-54; and learner input, 54-55; relevancy in, 52-53; television in, 13-15
Adult Learning Service, 16
Aggen, W., 99
Agraval, B. C., 15, 17
AGRICOLA, 35
Alaska, University of, telecourses from, 12
Alcoa, and interactive video, 36
Allen, D., 93, 98
Allen, F., 94, 99
American Association of Medical Colleges, 98
American Broadcasting Companies (ABC), 14
Anchorage Community College, and radio, 24
Andrews, D., 96, 99
Andrews, D. C., 57, 60
Annenberg, W., 16
Annenberg/Corporation for Public Broadcasting Project, 26, 43, 45
Artificial intelligence (AI), concept of, 55
Aslanian, C. B., 5, 8
Association for Media-Based Continuing Education for Engineers (AMCEE), 10
Athabasca University, correspondence course teams at, 46
Atlanta, telecourses from, 10
Audio: and access, 102, 105; analysis of potential of, 19-28; background on, 19-20; benefits of, 20-21; characteristics of, 20-21; and cooperation, 104; future of, 26-27; and learning strategies, 103; limitations of, 22-23, 25; radio as, 21-24; recordings as, 24-26; and teleconferencing, 26

Australia: correspondence education in, 43; persistence studies in, 83

B

Baath, J. A., 74, 80, 85
Bardwell, R., 82, 83, 85
Barker, J. A., 60, 61
Bates, A. W., 13, 18, 21, 24, 25, 27, 77-78, 85
Bayard-White, C., 35, 40
Bender, K. R., 55-56, 61
Blackburn, R. T., 27
Bloomsburg University, interactive video training at, 38
Bosco, J., 35, 40
Boston University, video transmission from, 10
Bove, L., 35, 39, 40
Bowlay, D. J., 83, 85
Breuer, K., 76, 80, 87
Brickell, H. M., 5, 8
Bridgman, D., 94, 99
Brigham Young University, and distance education, 42
Brittain, C. V., 80, 85
Brown, D., 78, 85
Brown, J., 96, 100
Brown, L., 11, 18
Bruno, R., 92, 99
Brush, D., 11, 18
Brush, J., 11, 18
Business training, computers and, 56-57
Butler, B., 31, 33, 40

C

Cable Television Network, 10
California, University of, and distance education, 42
California State University at Sacramento, video transmission from, 10
Canada: correspondence education in, 43, 46; open university in, 43; support services in, 84

109

Carnegie grants, 43
Carr, R., 97, 99
Carrier, C. A., 32, 51, 54, 61, 62, 102, 104, 105, 107
Center for the Study of Testing, Evaluation, and Educational Policy (CSTEEP), 27
Chicago, University of, and distance education, 42
Chicago Board of Education, and radio, 23
Chicago TV College, 15
Child, J., 10
Childs, G. B., 12, 18
China, People's Republic of, telecourses in, 15
Christensen, D., 98, 100
Church, F., 30-31
Clark, R. E., 77, 85
Cleveland, H., 63, 72
Cleveland, community computer in, 93
Coastline Community College, and television, 13
Cohen, A. A., 77, 87
Cohen, V. B., 83, 85
Colombia, television in, 15
Computer-Assisted Distance Education (CADE), and monitoring progress, 79
Computer-assisted learning (CAL), Merlin system for, 80-82
Computer-based instruction (CBI), and interactive video, 32
Computers: and access, 102, 105; in adult education, 52-55; analysis of roles for, 51-62; background on, 51-52; and business training, 56-57; and continuing education, 55-56; and disabled persons, 57-58; and human contact, 107; and learning strategies, 103; and motivation, 104; potentials and limitations of, 58-60; as writing tools, 57
Consortium for Telecommunication in Learning, 45
Content: nonprint media presentation of, 77-79; print media presentation of, 74-77
Continuing education, and computers, 55-56
Corporation for Public Broadcasting, 16, 18, 26, 43, 45

Costa Rica, open university in, 43
Creighton University, and satellite programming, 10

D

Dartmouth College, and microcomputers, 52
Davison, J., 74, 86
Daynes, R., 31, 33, 40
Deakin University, and correspondence education, 43
Demographic data, and learning outside the classroom, 4, 7
Detroit, literacy programs in, 14
Digital Equipment Corporation: Adaptive Learning Solutions (ALS) of, 36; and interactive video, 32, 33; Interactive Video Information System (IVIS) of, 56
Disabled persons, and computers, 57-58
Distance education: analysis of using technology in, 89-100; centralization and communication in, 90; commonalities in, 89-91; concept of, 42; conclusion on, 98; design guidelines for, 95-98; guided didactic conversation in, 44; humans and technology in, 89-90, 96, 106-107; hypermedia in, 94; as individualized and group, 90, 104; instructional designs for, 93-95; motivations for developing, 90-91; parallel systems in, 94-95; print media as, 41-42; scenario-based instruction for, 93-94; technological developments for, 91-93
Du Page, College of, and radio, 24
Durbridge, N., 20, 27

E

Eastman Kodak Company, Customer Service Division of, 56
Education, concept of, 20
Education Utility, as integrated information technology, 64-67
Educational Products Information Exchange, 60
Eurich, N. P., 56, 57, 61
Evans, R. E., 12, 18

111

F

Feedback: informational, 82-83; for knowledge of results, 82; for support, 83-84
Fernuniversitat, and distance education, 44, 46

G

Gagne, R., 96, 99
Gallagher, M., 76, 86
Gaynor, P., 83, 86
GED, and television, 14
Geest, D., 92, 99
George Washington University, video transmission from, 10
German, Federal Republic of: and distance education, 44, 46; open university in, 43; telecourses in, 15
Ging, T., 27
Glossbrenner, A., 63, 72
Goodson, L., 96, 99
Gooler, D. D., 1, 63, 67, 72, 92, 101, 102, 104, 107, 108
Grunder, T., 93, 99
Guided didactic conversation: in distance education, 44; in print media, 75-76

H

Hanafin, M., 54, 61
Harrington, H., 9, 18
Hartley, J. R., 82, 86
Hawkridge, D., 9, 13, 18, 64, 72
Heerman, B., 55, 61
Held, T., 99
Hess, R. D., 33, 40
Higher education: distance education in, 42-50; radio in, 23-24; television in, 15-17
Holbrook, D., 42, 50
Holmberg, B., 13, 18, 44, 50, 75, 76, 80, 83, 86
Hong Kong, open university in, 43
Houle, C. O., 19, 28
Hutson, B., 94, 100

I

IBM: and interactive video, 33; training by, 56

India, television in, 15
Indiana, video programming, in, 10
Indiana, University of, and distance education, 42
Information technologies, integrated: and access, 102, 105; analysis of, 63-72; benefits of, 67-69; conclusion on, 71-72; defining, 63-64; example of, 64-67; issues in use of, 69-71; and learning strategies, 103
Instructional functions: analysis of, 73-87; background on, 73-74; conclusion on, 84-85; of content presentation, 74-79; of feedback provision, 82-84; of monitoring progress, 79-82
Instructional Television Fixed Service (ITFS), 10, 11, 12
Instructor, and print media, 49-50
Intelligent computer-assisted instruction (ICAI), 55
Interactive video: and access, 102, 105; analysis of role of, 29-40; applications of, 34-37; background on, 29-31; design requirements for, 33-34; developing designers for, 38; evolving technologies for, 32-33; and human contact, 107; for independent learning, 35-36; interactivity levels of, 31-32, 37; and learning strategies, 103; potentials and limitations of, 38-40; and quality, 105; repurposing old media for, 36-37; technical characteristics of, 31-34; for traditional teaching, 36
International Council on Correspondence Education, 42
International University Consortium for Telecommunications in Learning, 43
Iowa, teleconferencing in, 26
Iowa, State University of, television at, 15
Israel: open university in, 43; telecourses in, 15
Italy, telecourses in, 15
Ixion, and interactive video, 37

J

Japan, open university in, 43
Johnson, D. W., 54, 61

Johnson, K. A., 1, 29, 40, 56, 102, 104, 105, 107
Johnson, R. T., 54, 61
Johnstone, J., 42, 50
Jones, A., 87

K

Kare, G. R., 44, 50
Kaufman, D., 73, 86
Keenan, J. M., 77, 87
Keller, J. M., 54, 61
Kelly, P., 25, 28
Kentucky, University of, microcomputers at, 56
Kentucky Educational Television (KET), 14
Kern, L., 21, 24, 27, 76, 86
Kerr, S., 97, 99
Kidd, J. R., 52, 61
Kingsland, L., 95, 99
Knapper, C. K., 73, 86
Knowles, M. S., 52, 61
Knox, A. B., 52, 61
Krisak, N., 52-53, 58, 61
Ksobiech, K., 77, 86
Kurland, M., 77, 86

L

Lagos, University of, Correspondence and Open Studies Institute at, 43
Larsen, R. E., 56, 61
Lavell, K., 82, 86
Law, M., 74, 76, 86
Learning: concept of, 20; emphasis on, 5-6, 7; independent, 35-36; lifelong, 6; right to, 6; self-directed, 5
Learning outside the classroom: audio technologies for, 19-28; computers for, 51-62; and demographic data, 4, 7; forces on technologies for, 3-8; implications for, 7-8; information technologies for, 63-72, 89-100; and instructional functions, 73-87; interactive video for, 29-40; issues and themes in, 101-108; and learning emphasis, 5-6, 7; and life transitions, 4-5, 7; and lifelong learning, 6; with print media, 41-50; television for, 9-18
Lent, R., 33, 40

Lentz, T. M., 12, 18
Lepper, M., 95, 99
Lewis, R. J., 27, 28
Lindberg, D., 95, 99
Literacy, and television, 13-14, 15
Little, D., 19, 20, 28
Locatis, C., 1, 89, 100, 103, 104, 105, 107
Lockheed, M., 97, 99
Lohman, D., 95, 100
London, J., 5, 8
Louisiana State University, and distance education, 42
Lowe, L., 92, 99

M

Mabry, F., 94, 100
McCombs, B. L., 53, 61
McCorduck, P., 63, 72
McCormick, D., 52-53, 58, 61
McDaniels, M. A., 53, 61
MacDonald-Ross, M., 44, 50, 75, 86
MacLachlan, J., 96, 99
Malone, T., 95, 99
Mandinach, E., 97, 99
Mansson, N. O., 80, 85
Marchesano, L., 57, 61
Marland, P. W., 75, 86
Maryland, University of: Center for Instructional Development and Evaluation (CIDE) at, 35, 37; and television, 13; video transmission from, 10
Maryland at College Park, University of, College of Library and Information Services at, 35
Maryland Public Broadcasting, 14
Merlin, evaluation studies of, 80-82
Merrill, M. D., 77, 86
Michael Reese Hospital and Medical Center, and computers, 55
Microsoft Press, 60
Miller, D., 91, 99
Minnesota, University of, and distance education, 42
Mississippi, University of, computers and correspondence courses at, 55-56
Mississippi Educational Television, 14
Missouri, University of, and distance education, 42

Mizushima, M., 92, 99
Montana, teleconferencing in, 26
Moore, M. G., 1, 41, 50, 103
Moran, T., 97, 99
Moses, S., 5, 8
Mozes, G., 55, 61
Munshi, K. S., 16, 18
Murphy, P., 87

N

National Agriculture Library (NAL), and interactive video, 35
National Cash Register Company: and interactive video, 33; training by, 56
National Information Utilities Corporation, 64
National Public Radio, 22
National Technological University (NTU), and training, 56
National University Consortium, 16
National University Teleconference Network (NUTN), 10
Nebraska: teleconferencing in, 26; Videodisc Award in, 37
Nebraska, University of: and distance education, 42; and interactive video, 31
Nelson, T., 94, 99
Netherlands, open university in, 43
Nevada, teleconferencing in, 26
New Jersey, cable network in, 10
New York Manpower Institute, 14
Niemi, J. A., 1, 3, 8, 101, 108
Niger, television in, 15
Nigeria, correspondence education in, 43
Nugent, R. W., 31, 34, 40

O

Ohio State University, and radio, 24
Oklahoma State University, teleconferences from, 10
Open Learning Institute: and correspondence education, 43; and support services, 84
Open University: computer-assisted learning at, 80; development of, 42-43; Institute of Education Technology (IET) of, 45, 75; and print media, 41, 43, 44, 46, 48, 50; and quality, 106; and radio, 21, 22, 23, 27, 78; and recordings, 25; and television, 15; and tutors, 106
Orndorff, J. E., 9, 18
O'Shea, T., 87

P

Pakistan, open university in, 43
Papert, S., 77, 86
Park, S., 98, 100
Patton, G. S., 94
Pea, R., 77, 86
Pennsylvania State University: and cable network, 10; Department of Independent Study by Correspondence (DISC) at, 45; and distance education, 42
Perkins, D., 98, 99
Perraton, H., 48, 50
Perrin, D. G., 12, 18
Peters, Professor, 46
Philadelphia, literacy series in, 13
Poland, telecourses in, 15
Portland, radio in, 23
Pratt, D. D., 1, 73, 86, 87, 103, 105
Print media: and access, 102, 105; analysis of, 41-50; characteristics of, 41-42, 47; content presentation by, 74-77; course design for, 45-49; as distance education, 41-42; guided didactic conversation in, 75-76; history of recent, 42-43; and instructor, 49-50; learner contribution to, 49; and learning strategies, 103; personality of, 48; research on, 44-45; self-sufficiency of, 48; structure of, 47-48; summary on, 50
Public Broadcasting Service (PBS), 10, 14
Purdie, L., 9, 18

R

Radio, potential of, 21-24
Raised Dot Computing, 58
Recordings, potential of, 24-26
Reeves, T., 93, 99
Reinhold, F., 52, 61
Reischmann, J., 20, 28
Riccobono, J., 23-24, 28

Rio Salada Community College, and teleconferencing, 26
Rivera, R., 42, 50
Roberts, F. C., 55, 61
Rogers, C., 74
Rogers, S., 52-53, 58, 61
Roper, W. J., 83, 86
Ross, S., 20, 28
Roszak, T., 70, 72
Rusnell, D., 84, 86
Rutkowski, C., 97, 99
Ryan, S., 25, 28

S

Saettler, P., 15, 18
Sales, G., 54, 61
Salomon, G., 77, 85, 86-87, 98, 99
Satellite Communication for Learning Associated (SCOLA), 10
Satellite Instructional Television Experiment (SITE), 15
Scanlon, E., 80, 81, 87
Schramm, W., 9, 18
Schwen, T., 73, 87
Shakespeare, W., 76
Sharp, G., 95, 99
Shneiderman, B., 97, 100
Simpson, K., 56, 61
Sissons, L., 74, 76, 86
Sivatko, J., 42, 50
Skinner, B. F., 74
Sleeman, D., 96, 100
Smart, K., 44, 50
Smith, K. C., 45, 50
Snow, R., 95, 100
Sokoloff, M., 61
Source, 64
Spain, open university in, 43
Sri Lanka, open university in, 43
Stanford University, video transmission from, 10
Stone, D., 94, 100
Store, R. E., 75, 86
Subsidiary Communications Authorization (SCA), 22, 24
Sweden, monitoring progress in, 79

T

Takemoto, P. A., 1, 19, 28, 102, 104
Tatum, R., 91, 100
Taylor, F. J., 44, 50

Technology: and access and equity issues, 8, 59, 70, 102-103, 105; audio, 19-28; benefits of, 101-105; and channel capacity, 91; computers as, 51-62; concept of, 73; conclusion on, 107; design guidelines for, 95-98; forces on, 3-8; and humans, in distance education, 89-90, 96, 106-107; impact of, 3-4, 8; implications for use of, 7-8; and individualized and group instruction, 90, 104; instructional designs for, 93-95; and instructional functions, 73-87; integrated information, 63-72; and integrated media, 92; interactive video for, 29-40; and interlinked systems, 92; issues and themes in, 101-108; and learning strategies, 103; limitations of, 105-107; and motivation to learn, 103-104; orientation to, 78-79; print media as, 41-50; prior experience with, 77-78; properties and potential of, 77; and quality issues, 105-106; and retrieval, 92-93; and storage capacity, 91; teaching with, 89-100; television as, 9-18; training users of, 107
Teleconferencing, potential of, 26
Television: and access, 102, 105; in adult education, 13-15; analysis of role of, 9-18; broadcast, 9-10; future of, 17; in higher education, 15-17; limitations of, 12-13; and literacy, 13-14, 15; narrowcast, 10; utilization of, 11-13; and videocassettes, 11; and viewer support system, 14-15
Telford, I., 94, 99
Tennyson, R., 98, 100
Tennyson, R. D., 76, 80, 87
Texas, video programming in, 10
Texas Technical University, and distance education, 42
Thailand, open university in, 43
Thomasson, J. E., 56, 61
Thrush, D., 94, 100
Tikomirov, O. K., 77, 87
Tough, A., 5, 8
Transmediation, and content presentation, 76-77
Tucker, M. S., 26, 28
Turle, S., 98, 100
Turkle, S., 63, 72

U

UNESCO, 6, 8
Union of Soviet Socialist Republics, telecourses in, 15
United Kingdom. See Open University
U.S. Air Force, and computer-based instruction, 53
U.S. Army, STARS program of, 93-94
U.S. Bureau of the Census, 4, 8
U.S. Navy, Health Services Command of, 36-37

V

Venezuela, open university in, 43
Video. See Interactive video
Vincent, T., 87

W

Walker, D. F., 33, 40
Waller, R., 75, 76, 87
Walshok, M. L., 13, 18
Washington, teleconferencing in, 26
Wedemeyer, C. A., 5, 8, 12, 18, 19, 28, 43
Wenkert, R., 5, 8
Wertheim, S., 94, 100
Western Reserve University, telecourses from, 15
Whitelegg, L., 87
Wiesner, P., 1, 9, 13, 18, 102, 105
Wilson, H., 42
Wilson Learning Corporation, Interactive Technology Group of, 56-57
Winner, L., 69-70, 72
Wisconsin, teleconferencing in, 26
Wisconsin, University of: Articulated Instructional Media (AIM) at, 42-43; and audio, 24, 26; and distance education, 42; television from, 14
Writing, computers as tools for, 57

X

Xerox Corporation, training by, 56

Z

Zemke, R., 52, 61
Zimler, J., 77, 87